Donna J. Arnink received an M.F.A. in production design from Ohio University. She has taught art to all grade levels and currently teaches design at Michigan State University Theater.

Creative
Theatrical
Makeup

Donna J. Arnink

*Visuals by Pat York, Sylvia Ryland,
Karleen Arnink, and Donna Arnink*

A SPECTRUM BOOK

Prentice-Hall, Inc., Englewood Cliffs, New Jersey 07632

Library of Congress Cataloging in Publication Data

Arnink, Donna J.
　Creative theatrical makeup.

　"A Spectrum Book."
　Includes index.
　1. Make-up, Theatrical.　I. York, Pat.　II. Title.
PN2068.A68　1984　　　792'.027　　　84–1610410 (pbk.)
ISBN 0–13–191313–1
ISBN 0–13–191305–0 pbk.

This book is available at a special discount when ordered in bulk quantities.
Contact Prentice-Hall, Inc., General Publishing Division,
Special Sales, Englewood Cliffs, N. J. 07632

ISBN 0-13-191313-1

ISBN 0-13-191305-0 {PBK.}

Cover design: Hal Siegel
Manufacturing: Anne P. Armeny
Production coordination: Inkwell

Prentice-Hall International, Inc., *London*
Prentice-Hall of Australia Pty. Limited, *Sydney*
Prentice-Hall Canada Inc., *Toronto*
Prentice-Hall of India Private Limited, *New Delhi*
Prentice-Hall of Japan, Inc., *Tokyo*
Prentice-Hall of Southeast Asia Pte. Ltd., *Singapore*
Whitehall Books Limited, *Wellington, New Zealand*
Editora Prentice-Hall do Brasil Ltda., *Rio de Janeiro*

Contents

Makeup Products, 165

Preface

The ideal makeup artist has the eye of the caricaturist, the hands of the sculptor, the brush of the portrait painter, and the curiosity of the student. —*Greer Garson*

Despite the fact that theatrical makeup and art have repeatedly been aligned over the years, performers—struggling with their greasepaints, sponges, and brushes—rarely consider themselves artists. Unfortunately, in classes and in front of the mirror, makeup seems to be embraced more as a mere process than an art, passed by rote from seasoned performer to novice, or often simply copied from the pages of a book.

Makeup *should* be considered an art. Like all art—whether painting, sculpture, ceramics, graphics, architecture, or scenography—makeup relies on the basics of line, shape, texture, color, and composition for its success.

With a background as an art teacher, an actress, and a portrait painter, I was admittedly frustrated at what I had experienced in the realm of theatrical makeup when I first began teaching it over a decade ago. It seemed only rational that the theories incorporated in applying pigment to linen canvas could be successfully adapted to the human canvas, resulting in a more natural-looking, creative expression of character and general enhancement.

Consequently, a new approach to teaching and applying cosmetics for the stage took form. Classes stressed art techniques, while the application process itself adopted a drastic departure from the usual approaches with "instant complexions" found in tubes and tins of pancake. Pure color, used as portrait artists have employed it for centuries, was incorporated to provide a more exciting and believable appearance on stage.

I must admit to being a bit skeptical myself as that first class abandoned their greasepaints and pancakes in lieu of a color palette. The enthusiasm and dedication shown by those first dozen brave souls were gratifying. The students not only conquered color, but they were having a ball to boot! A greater appreciation of art was evident, providing an expanded means of expression. Most rewarding, each saw him- or herself as more of an artist, with new esteem and seriousness for the "art" of theatrical makeup.

Subsequent terms were used to evaluate the color approach versus the more traditional application in a variety of situations. We found that color read with more clarity and believability in long-play situations as well as in film and television. The black students were thrilled, as the color system enabled them to develop a flexibility and range not possible with standard approaches. And *all* the students were pleased that the makeup kit—composed of only five colors, a sponge, and brush—was reduced not only in volume, but in cost as well!

The course has expanded over the years with the system being introduced in workshops throughout the country, and the response has been enthusiastic. This "bizarre" manner of making up has become logical and commonplace for hundreds of performers, students, and makeup artists who have either adopted it in its entirety or integrated it with more conventional systems.

This book promotes the philosophy of makeup as a true art, providing information and exercises that will help readers understand this important correlation, as well as develop skills that will enable them to design more creative and complete makeup. It is hoped that the present reader, like so many students of this theory in the past, will find this route not only thorough and innovative, but most enjoyable as well.

Lots of hugs and sincere thanks to Pat and Judy for all their support and assistance. Thanks, Ramona, for your patience, and special and heartfelt appreciation to all of the students whose time and energy made this publication a reality.

1

Makeup as Art

The curious power of the facial image over the artistic imagination is perhaps most clearly shown by the central role that masks and makeup have played in social history. Since the very dawn of self-discovery, civilizations have embraced the human form as a living canvas to be stenciled, painted, decoratively scarred, and lavishly adorned. Like a lateral fiber, the practice has submerged and resurfaced throughout time in a closely knit expression of religious beliefs, ritual, fashion, and social status.

Being a reflection of society, the theatre was, up until only a century ago, simply a mirror for all this fickle, fad, and fancy. Greek masks were painted to duplicate contemporary fashion in makeup. Medieval theatre, adhering to strict religious atmosphere that forbade makeup of any kind, utilized no makeup beyond a bit of red stain for the actor who portrayed the devil character. The theatre of Shakespeare's era found the performers using no makeup beyond that which was found in general society, a practice that continued until a change in the physical theatre demanded it in the late 1800s. Electric lights, the reliance on footlights, and large

1

ANCIENT

Figure 1–1.
The ancients were very fashion conscious. The Kamasutra devoted no less than 65 chapters to body beautification, including the painting of hair, nails, and teeth! Cosmetics have been unearthed in archeological digs and tombs dating back thousands of years, while paintings and statues confirm that both the male and female decorated themselves lavishly. The Assyrians took great pride in their appearances, bleaching their faces with white lead. Since baldness was often considered a curse in ancient civilizations, wigs of goat hair were popular, as were false beards (even for women of nobility). Those who sported a full head of hair curled it tightly with curling irons and dusted it with gold powder.

The well-coiffed Persians favored eye makeup, creating dark islands of kohl liner on their whitened faces. They applied this blackener so heavily to their brows that they often connected into one languished line across their forehead!

The Egyptians, known for their lavish cosmetics, beauty oils, and perfumes, were veritable walking paintings. Both sexes whitened their faces with ceruse and lined their eyes with black kohl. In addition, eye pastes of blue and green circled the eye, contrasting with cheeks of yellow ochre and bright red lips. Faint rivers of blue stain followed the veins on the chest, and exposed nipples were painted gold! Even the hands and feet were attended to, as henna dyes were often applied to turn them an attention-getting crimson.

darkened theatres required a thick, obvious application of cosmetics. Lacking in expressive charm or characterization, a mask-like application outraged the Victorian moralists, who quickly lumped actors into the same disrespectful category as harlots and criminals. Despite the disfavor, however, theatrical makeup was here to stay, starting a swing that would take this expressive device into a realm of its own.

Figure 1–2.
Throughout history, it has been the male of the species who has generally gone to the greatest lengths of adornment. The Greeks were no exception. The most popular gathering place in ancient Greece was undoubtedly the equivalent to our modern barber and health salons. It was here that the Greek males, young and old alike, gathered daily to share news, discuss events, listen to poetry, and debate philosophical matters. In addition, the Greek man could have his beard trimmed, his locks curled, his fingers and toes manicured, and his entire body massaged. The Greeks powdered their faces, utilized paints on their eyes, cheeks, and lips, and often wore wreaths of flowers in their hair. During the Homeric period, full beards were popular and often curled. The Periclean age brought about a generally clean-shaven look to the young males, with makeup and hair styles of great similarity between the sexes. Later, as facial hair became equated with barbarism, Alexander forbade his soldiers to grow facial hair and required short hair styles. While retaining their cosmetics, the Greek males adopted short curls and clean-shaven faces. Only an occasional patch of long hair was seen, hanging in front of the ear.

GREEK

ROMAN

Figure 1–3.
The Greeks were outdone by the Romans in their fervor for personal beauty. The "barber shops" of Rome offered not only steam baths, manicures, cuts, plucking, trims, depilatory treatments and massages, but wine and women as well. The Romans were fastidious in their daily toilet, heaping scorn on those who were not impeccably adorned or those whose makeup had run in the heat. Though women, particularly courtesans, strove for beautification equal to the men, philosophers of the period noted (rather disdainfully) that their "art wanted for perfection." Both sexes pumiced their teeth for whiteness, bathed in asses' milk for soft skin, darkened their eyes and lashes with kohl and colors, and whitened their faces fashionably. Introduced were leather patches of various shapes and sizes that were adhered to the face to hid blemishes. Men were obsessed with their hair. Blond locks were considered a gift from the gods, and baldness was still considered a curse. Consequently, their hair was frequently bleached or blond wigs were worn. Often, in the absence of any hair, curls were simply painted on!

Theatrical makeup as a creative art was stalled for decades amid the fervor of dramatic thinking that bridged theatre into the twentieth century. Churning with artistic revolution, scenic designers departed from realism to embrace the abstract and emotionally induced. For the first time, artists designed costumes for specific roles. Scenic artists experimented in new realms, while the "art" of makeup puttered along in the dust raised by design innovations in other areas. Left to individual interpretation and application, the thickly applied "mask," with its gaudily colored accents, played on.

MEDIEVAL

Figure 1–4.

Fad and fashion faded with the fall of the Roman Empire, to lay dormant until the crusades, when the oils, perfumes, and cosmetics brought back from the conquests gave rise to their popularity once more. Prostitutes adopted makeup first, and though the church was violently opposed to any type of adornment, cosmetics soon spread to the masses. The Medieval woman shaved her head and whitened her face, and though the church advocated that red was a sign of a witch, the popularity of reddened cheeks and lips soon made this association inconsequential. Bright wigs were worn, again in opposition to the church, which advocated that the evil spirits of a person remained in the hair, regardless of who was wearing it! The religious faction was ignored on every front, however, in the new fashion fervor. It is said that Isabeau, queen of France, was covered daily with a powerful beauty potion of boar's brains, crocodile glands, and wolf blood, at which time an alchemist chanted incantations over her. Shoulder-length hair was popular on men by the 12th century. Both men and women "crisped" the ends of their hair with curling irons at this time. The 13th century saw short hair and beards rise in popularity. The "page boy" came into fashion, along with other rolled styles. Women wore their hair uncut, pulled back into braids, and tied up in various styles. By 1450, hair was curled in curl papers and continued to be crisped. Men wore ribbons, while older men wore beards. The "bowl cut" was popular, a circular trim resembling a bowl that left a fringe of hair around the head. Silk wigs were available in colors including bright yellow, and anyone who had the misfortune to have red hair, readily dyed or powdered it.

1500s

Figure 1–5.
Wigs were still popular in the 1500s. Elizabeth is said to have had over sixty, and poor Mary Stuart, while imprisoned in the tower, reportedly changed hers daily. Fancy beards abounded, pressed into wooden devices by night to hold their shape. Fancy pointed beards became popular from the Spanish influence by the end of the century. Lovelocks, often decorated with ribbons or beads, were favored by males. Wire frames at the temples supported curls and fancy hair arrangements. Mixtures of white paste of ceruse and egg were thickly applied to the face and "fixed" there with a thin mixture of shellac. It is doubtful that people changed expressions for fear of their faces cracking. (In fact, it is doubtful that they could change expression.) Men blackened their eyebrows and plucked them, and face painting was popular with both sexes. Abrasive mixtures were concocted to "sand" away blemishes. In addition, cosmetics were used that were high in poison content and consequently etched away the skin and corroded the hair. Hence, women's eyebrows disappeared and the hairline retreated several inches, creating the high forehead so popular in Medieval days. Cartouches (love patches) again became popular to hide the abused complexion. Samuel Pepys mentioned in his famous diary that his wife certainly looked beautiful when he gave her leave to wear black patches to cover the pimples about her mouth! The barber shop surged back into popularity at this time, providing entertainment, social stimulus, music, and personal care as had been enjoyed in ancient times. In addition, services were rendered that included blood-letting and tooth pulling!

1600s

Figure 1–6.
When King Louis XIII began losing his hair because of illness, wigs, which had fallen into disfavor, instantly became the rage. Hundreds of wig-makers populated Paris alone. Cascades of free-flowing curls were quite popular on males, as were the stylish "lovelocks" with their decorations of ribbons or flowers. With the exception of a tiny moustache, facial hair virtually disappeared on all but old men. Women's styles in both wigs and natural hair included rolling, twisting, or braiding the hair on the top or back of the head, allowing ringlets of hair to fall freely on the shoulders. Ribbons or beads were often used as adornment. Patches became popular once more, as it became fashionable to "speak" through them. One's political views could be ascertained by the position of a patch, as could a young woman's availability. The length to which this practice was carried is emphasized by a period engraving that depicts, among other decorations, a large coach pulled by an entire team of horses galloping across a woman's forehead, nearly obliterating her face completely! In addition to patches of silk or leather, decorations were painted directly onto the face for the truly fashionable look.

1700s

Figure 1–7.
The 18th century found patches and paints still quite in fashion, particularly for men. Hair demanded the most attention, however. While long heavy curls were out of style, every imaginable arrangement replaced them. Natural hair and wigs alike were frequently pulled back into pigtails that either hung loose or were encased in a silk bag. Powdering was definately "in," and powders of various colors were either shot directly onto the hair with bellows or aimed into the air and allowed to fall on the wearer. It is said that the average revolutionary soldier used over a pound a week to maintain a stylish demeanor. Combing the hair became a popular public pastime, with the theatre being the most favored spot to demonstrate this talent. By 1770 wigs had become so outlandish that elaborate wire frames were needed to support them. Women wore veritable sculptures atop their heads, with everything but the proverbial kitchen sink floating in their tresses. The church became so alarmed at the extent to which makeup and wigs had advanced that they passed penalties equal to those for sorcery and witchcraft on any woman who seduced a man into marriage through such fabrications. It was the eventual association of the wig with the hated aristocracy in Europe that marked its decline. A more natural look prevailed at the end of the century when the "brutus crop," a faddish look, was adopted. This hair style was a disheveled arrangement adopted by both sexes. Beau Brummel appeared on the scene at this time, advocating outrageous new standards in cleanliness by bathing daily, brushing his teeth, and washing his hair every two weeks! "Natural" was "in."

1800s

Figure 1–8.
The early 19th century saw a movement to shorter, more natural hair styles for men. Curls and waves were the rage. Women largely abandoned wigs as well, and twisted, curled, and braided their own long hair, often decorating it with feathers or beads. Beards and moustaches grew in popularity toward the middle of the century, until it was rare to see a clean-shaven face. Thick facial growths, including the famous "Picadilly weeper" adorned the male face until the end of the century, when more conservative styles predominated. Dyes were popular throughout the century, including bright colors for facial hair as well as tresses. Though cosmetics were generally frowned upon by the dominant Victorian society, cosmetic manufacturers promoted a return to makeup by advertising their creams and colors as being useful for constipation, nausea, and headaches. Though the "pale look" was definitely in, it is doubtful that many women applied makeup to their faces for health reasons, and by the turn of the century, colored creams and powders again adorned the faces of men and women alike.

Figure 1–9.

The beginning of this century looked much like any other at first. Men were still frequenting the barber shops, where they were trimmed, manicured, and made up. Hair styles were relatively short, slightly curled or singed, and parted in the center. Except for older men, few males wore moustaches or beards. Then a revolutionary thing happened. Women invaded the barber shops! The famous "Gibson girl" look, so popular at the turn of the century, gave way to the scandalous short "bob" and the colorful world of speakeasies and flappers, where women donned the new artificial eyelashes and covered their faces with lavish cosmetics, dark powders, lipsticks, eye shadow, and penciled eyebrows. Beauty shops sprung up for women, providing the tight marcel wave that the men were receiving in the barber shops themselves in the 20s. Medium-length sweeps of dyed or rinsed hair, influenced by the movies, were popular for women in the 30s, while the "patent leather" look predominated for males. The 40s saw a popularity of soft waves, longer hair, and more fullness. By the 50s the male image had changed drastically. Men, who for centuries have reveled in the elegant look cosmetics provided, were now highly embarrassed at the thought of powdering or lining their eyes. Women, in a very short time, captured the cosmetic domain completely, and manufacturers responded with products and advertising directed to the female. The 50s also marked the beginning of the "trendy" fashion that continues today. A curious collage of styles in hair and makeup application, promoted by the fashion industry, incited by entertainment stars, or born of political or social protest, has blanketed the last several decades. The macho G.I. or "crew" cut collided with the long greasy look inspired first by Elvis Presley. The neat short styles so fashionable on college campuses in the early 60s gave way to the moppet look worn by the Beatles. Heavy makeup became the fashion, almost to the point of gaudiness in the early part of the 1960s. Ratted and teased hair thrived amidst the unkept, long-haired look inspired by the hippies. By the end of the 1960s makeup had moved toward the more natural look, and men were beginning to return to the barber shops, where barbers were recouping business by billing themselves as "stylists." From a decade of revolutionary expressions, the creative 70s emerged with an even greater variety of options. The lop-sided Sassoon, the tightly-permanented afro, and even long, perfectly straight tresses were popular. Uni-sex fashion was in, inspired by rock stars. Facial hair was extremely common on younger men in particular for the first time in this century. The emphasis on makeup altered from the obvious to the understated, with soft blush colors replacing the harsher cosmetics of the previous decade. The natural look was definitely promoted on every level with many women abandoning makeup altogether. The 80s moved in, carried by the punk movement, which advocates bizarre hair styles of various florescent colors, stick-on tattoos, and stark color contrasts in makeup. The preppie look reminiscent of the early 60s returned, advocating a clean, neat, bare-faced appearance. Short hair styles for both sexes, fashion model-inspired makeups for women, and a generally casual look predominate.

With no makeup artists or designers, actors and actresses turned to "how-to" books, which flooded the market. Reading much like pharmaceutical guides or anatomy journals, they offered little in the way of creative application . . . or even characterization. Suffering from a dearth of pictures, the texts laboriously explained step by step how to do Hamlet, Lear, or Falstaff. Stereotypes were the rule, and creativity was limited to recipes for greasepaints!

Makeup might have been mired in the mundane forever were it not for the growing arm of the entertainment industry. Nurtured by endless technical advances, the films moved like a steam roller into the hearts of Americans. Movies became the vehicle that finally provoked serious changes in the attitude toward and in the application of makeup.

Advanced systems of lighting, combined with the closeness with which the audience viewed the performer on the cinematic screen, demanded a standardization of this makeup application for all the members of a cast. This intimate situation made greasepaint appear in a grotesque manner and required new cosmetics that were lighter and thinner. The public's insatiable desire for the bizarre necessitated types of makeup never before seen by an audience or, for that matter, by the actors who found themselves playing a mutant from Mars, moon men, or a slimy amphibious creature who arose from a cinema sea to conquer the world. As a result, for the first time makeup artists were needed to coordinate, design, and actually apply makeup for all the members of the cast.

Virtually overnight, makeup came into an artistic realm of its own. The entertainers, the audiences, and the producers quickly realized the importance of creative and natural-looking makeup. Once it was recognized as an art, it was only natural that those men who quickly rose to the top of the profession were artists in their own right—painters, sculptors, jewelers, and graphic artists. The list includes such noted figures as Dick Smith (*Little Big Man*), John Chambers (*Planet of the Apes*), Rick Baker (*King Kong*), and Ben Nye (*The Fly*). Summing up their philosophy is Bill Tuttle, the Oscar-winning makeup artist responsible for the inventive makeups in *Young Frankenstein*. He urges the aspiring makeup artist to study life drawing, painting, and sculpture because they "all contribute to a basic knowledge that is necessary in any makeup process, be it simply beautification or characterization."

There is no doubt that the execution of makeup benefits greatly from artistically skilled hands and minds. However, the majority of legitimate theatres around the country, let alone small drama groups or educational producers, cannot afford the luxury of a professional makeup artist. The application of makeup is frequently done by an unskilled volunteer, an assigned committee, or, in most cases, the performers themselves. A dearth of time, artistic background, and application skills all contribute to makeup that often appears contrived and obvious. The obvious solution lies in training the performer, as well as novice makeup artists, in artistic skills that will enhance not only their application of makeup, but their capacity for character analysis and design.

"But I want to be an actor . . . not an artist!"

Designing makeup should be as much a part of actor preparation as movement and diction. The audience focuses on the performer's face for vital clues as to the character's age, life style, feelings, life experiences, and the like. An incredible amount of information can be conveyed by well designed makeup, enhancing the performer's body and voice.

"Me? Artistic? Why I can barely get my pancake on without smudging it."

Approaching makeup as an art implies learning basic fundamentals that will serve as building blocks for design and execution. It does not insist that every actor become a Norman Rockwell or a Picasso. Despite fears and misgivings, virtually *anyone* can develop a working artistic "vocabulary" that will assure better application and design of both straight and character makeups.

This book goes beyond the standard application techniques of "where" to put "what" in doing theatrical makeup, moving into the "whys" and "hows" that encompass all art, thus fusing the two. Though art techniques have been stressed in theatre makeup since Richard Corson's first book in 1940, they have never been fully explored and integrated into makeup design, thus providing the person who is applying makeup with a complete range of skills and confidence. This book intends to fill some of those gaps, while instilling an appreciation of art and its immediate application to the actor's face. The basic elements of art—line, form, and color—are explored in novel ways that provide an entirely new way of creating complexion tones and exciting characterizations. Exercises are suggested to help build artistic confidence, show the relationship between art and makeup, and illustrate the basic principles of visual perception.

The reader of this book is consistently referred to as the "makeup artist." This will establish the self-confidence that is important in approaching makeup design. No distinctions are used to divide the person who in fact wants a career of applying makeup from high school students who are applying their own makeup for the first time, or from professional performers who have been applying their own makeup for decades. Experience, in fact, does not always insure more successful makeup. Often, one "perfects" only the same old mistakes over the years, caught in the safety net of rote application. The artistic techniques supplied in the following chapters will provide fresh and exciting avenues of expression for both the novice and the professional.

2

Line

Line is a convenient discovery of humankind, not existing as such in nature, but its language of symbolism is more powerful than any written word. From the earliest cave dwellers, who utilized it to convey the animal forms they hunted, to the cartoonist who amuses us in the Sunday comics, this magic medium has served to communicate a universally recognizable syntax of human experience.

Of all the design tools (line, shape, color, composition, and texture), line is the most simple and fun to work with. Developing an awareness of its power will benefit the makeup artist not only in observing human features, but in designing forceful makeups that instill a convincing sense of personality and character.

From the first time we picked up a coloring book, we have been exposed to a linear language. Curvacious ribbons of black enclosed the form of a friendly sea creature or the cascading curls of a fairy princess. Thicker, heavier lines collided in sharp angles, defining a fearful monster or perhaps a nasty witch peering out from a sharply turreted castle.

After coloring books came comic books, then cartoons, textbooks, and television. We began to recognize the "bad guys" by the lines used to create them, just as we were attached to a

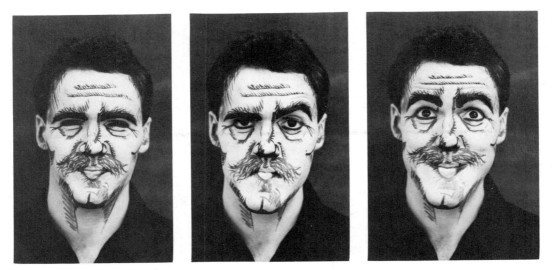

Figure 2–1.

Figure 2–2.
Even as children, we are influenced by a variety of lines and shapes.

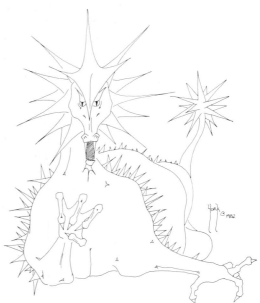

lovable cartoon character because of the way he or she was drawn. Thus, when we began to develop drawing skills to represent our life experiences, we automatically integrated this most familiar form of artistic signature.

Learning to "See"

Line is so basic a language that we understand its grammar without interpretation. To illustrate this, have a friend or two express the emotions joy, hate, sensuality, and loneliness on a piece of paper. Simply say each word and have them express each with an abstract line (with their eyes closed so they can "feel" the word). The results will always be surprisingly similar. Joy assumes a curly format with frequent upswings, while hate expresses itself with heavy, dark marks that entail points. While sensuality finds expression in softly curving lines of a static quality, loneliness is usually shown with a tiny dot or with a short horizontal line, often in the corner.

Figure 2–3.
Line is a more powerful force on our lives than we realize.

Joy

Anger

Eroticism

Loneliness

This simple exercise dictates a learned conditioning that was never taught in the classroom. Artists—be they architects, interior designers, advertising specialists, graphic designers, or cartoonists —are well "schooled" in line and human response, using the knowledge to carefully control consumer appeal. Wallpaper, cereal boxes, book covers, and even automobiles are designed with a particular appeal in mind.

Makeup artists have a similar responsibility in that their creations must "sell" the believability of a given character both to the performer who wears the cosmetic and to the audience observing the actor. The makeup artist can learn to utilize line in creating a character who is sweet, cunning, nasty, stupid, or insane.

The advantage of working in line is that we humans automatically ignore the volume and mass of any given object. An artist can draw only a few scribbles on paper and the viewer immediately envisions an entire face! This is because few of us actually "see" with the eyes, but rather with the mind, which readily supplies all the information it knows "should" be there. Using line to see what one is really looking at is an important step in being able to observe and analyze human faces. The makeup artist has to build a repertoire of physical features—certain types and expressions—so that they can be recalled and utilized in creating truly expressive makeup. The more detail one learns to see, the easier it will be to draw and paint . . . both on paper and on the human face.

A quick exercise to illustrate this principle will teach you a great deal about artistic observation. It also takes the pressure off doing pretty, pleasing, or perfect pictures, placing the emphasis where it should be—on ingesting vital visual information about the human face.

Face a friend, sketchbooks in hand, and draw one another's portrait. *However*, don't allow yourselves to look at the paper . . . even once! Instead, concentrate on your eye movements as they flow over each feature on the face, dip on the lower eyelid, slide down a nasalabial crease, or wind their way over each hair in the eyebrow. Imagine that a string is stretched tautly between your retina and your pencil so that every movement, every angle is duplicated exactly. The eye and hand should move in perfect synchronization. Move slowly, making mental calculations of proportions and relationships. If you must pick up your pencil, "feel" the

Figure 2–4.
Though not exactly a gallery piece, this
type of drawing teaches one to "see" with
more accuracy and detail.

proportional distance to the nose or the chin and move your pencil without glancing downward at your paper. Only when you are done may you look at the result.

   Granted, this might not be exactly the kind of picture you'd want hanging on your refrigerator, but they are a lot of fun to do. They tend to make people more comfortable about their artistic abilities, and, after all, from this point they can only improve! Of course, what has actually transpired is more important than the scrawlings on the paper imply. The eyes have programmed a very exact rendering on the tableau of the mind. Renderings of this sort, whether they be self-portraits to learn more about one's own face or street sketches of interesting people, provide lots of information that can be cataloged and utilized when designing character sketches for roles.

Cartooning for Expression

The next step entails the manipulation of line to intentionally create character—or cartooning. It allows one to focus on the most essential elements that cue us to emotions, or personality. Think for a moment of your favorite cartoons, and apply them to the exercise on joy, hate, and the other emotions. The type of line usually denotes the character of the cartoon figure. The Schultz gang are all composed of circular, "joyous" lines, while the nasty types that populate the world of Dick Tracy are drawn with heavy, angular lines. Collect examples of cartoons or comics to aid in the next exercise.

Figure 2–5.

a

b

c

d

e

f

g

h

Figure 2–6.

Place half a dozen ovals on a sheet of paper and write various emotions, personality types, or situations beneath them. Examples might be "Snooty," "Wicked," "Stupid thug," "Dumb blonde," or provocations such as "Your puppy was just run over by a truck." Use someone with a flexible face and a propensity for hamming it up as a model. First observe how the features lay in a relaxed state. Trace carefully in your mind the line of the mouth, the angle of the eyebrow, any pronounced wrinkles, and the placement of the nasalabial fold. Then ask your model to respond to each word and observe the dramatic change in the face. Because such an exaggerated pose is difficult to maintain, try to capture the expression as quickly as possible. Concentrate on the particular features that denote the expression rather than hair, ears, or often the nose.

Figure 2–7.
Can you see from these finished makeups how they were influenced by the original cartoon characters?

a

b

c

d

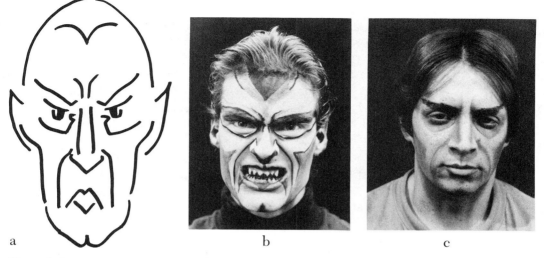

Figure 2–8.
Though stylized makeup benefits most immediately from a cartoon approach, more realistic makeups can have their impetus in cartoons as well.

Cartoon as many expressions as you or your model can think of. Each will contribute a little more information to be cataloged on paper and in your mind as well.

Cartooning characters as one studies a script can result in some delightful ideas, which can benefit even fairly "straight" characters. Whimsical, fantastic, or stylized roles can often be taken immediately from the cartoons. Figures 2–7a and b illustrate two cartoons done by a makeup artist to convey her attitude about two characters in a childrens' production. One was a dull, nasty "bad guy," while his sidekick was a very dopey, rather likable sort. These sketches provided the impetus for a lively dialogue among the actors, the director, and the designers, which helped clarify the roles more clearly. Figure 2–7c and d show the completed makeups. One can see the influence of the cartoons, though each has been expanded in volume and color.

The cartoon in Figure 2–8a indicates a character who is evil and nasty. Figures 2–8b and c illustrate two approaches done from the cartoon idea. The first retains more of the linear approach found in the cartoon, giving it a particularly stylized appearance, while the second, though still exaggerated, has a more realistically playable appearance.

The clown in Figure 2–9a expresses the particularly sad look originally created from the cartoon in Figure 2–9b.

When a line connects with itself, it forms a particular shape which is governed by the visual rules that determine our response to line. A circle or oval composed of curved lines, for instance, creates a happy look, while angular shapes like a triangle create a harsh look. (Note the subtle triangular shapes in Figure 2–9a.) The actress in Figures 2–10a through d has divided her face into areas using curved shapes on one side and angular configurations on the other. Note how severe the angular side looks in comparison to the "friendly" side. Even blending these areas, as one might do for stage distance, fails to diminish the effect.

Figure 2–9.

a

b

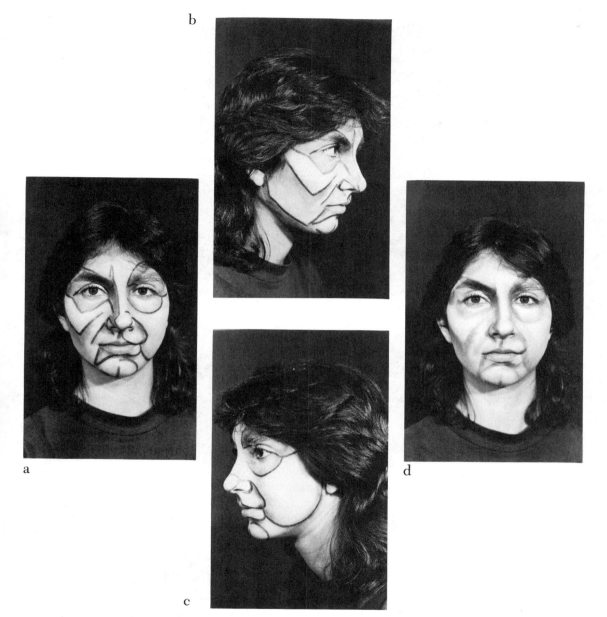

b

a

c

d

Figure 2–10.
A sensitive choice of line and shape will contribute greatly to the overall appearance of the performer.
Circular shapes lend a pleasant, friendly personality, while harsher angles create a more severe look.

Figure 2–11.
This stylized makeup benefits
directly from the use of circular
shapes on the face.

Figure 2–12.
Though more subtle, the
circular motif adds a jolly sense
to this character.

Figures 2–11 and 2–12 show two characters done with a circular approach in line and shape. These makeups certainly have a more inviting presence than those in Figures 2–8b and c.

Drawing with Proportions

Regardless of how realistic or how stylized one designs, line is certainly a valuable consideration and departure point. So far, we have encouraged line to be a free form expression, not limited by proportions and scale. Drawing without boundries frees the artistic mind to be more creative, unencumbered by rules and regulations. One would never need to progress beyond this point if makeup was designed for beach balls, nerf dolls, or blobs of silly putty. One would need only to push a little here or deflate a little there to create a shape that would conform to that indicated by the drawing. Unfortunately, the human face is not so pliable. It is very important in drawing preliminary sketches and facial maps that the ideas presented can in fact be transferred with accuracy to the features. If one cannot sketch a face with at least some degree of accuracy, preplanned modifications, alterations, or even the simple reinforcement of features could prove very disappointing when copied onto a real face. It is very easy to make a chin look three inches longer in a sketchpad. It is often quite another thing to create these effects on a three-dimensional feature.

The last exercise in this chapter suggests an easy way to use line in a representational way. Scale, relationships, and proportions are already mapped out. You need only to utilize your new skills in seeing to "fill in the blanks." This type of drawing is called a "contour" drawing since only lines define the various contours of each facial feature. In essence, it is a "no peeking" problem in which you are encouraged to look!

Though standardized forms of the basic female and male heads are often provided on which to plan one's makeup, having a self-portrait is much more useful. By making photocopies and planning makeup application on them, one can be assured of great accuracy and control.

Figure 2–13.
This lovely rendering by Leonardo Da Vinci captures expressions wonderfully.
Many of the sketches done by the old masters in preparing their canvases for
painting can be a rich source of ideas for character development. By the gracious
permission of her majesty Queen Elizabeth II.

For some people, working from a photograph, since it is already a flat two-dimensional form, is easier than drawing from a mirror. If you choose to work this way, however, keep a mirror handy since important detail is often vague in a photo. Since you will also need a profile sketch (one can't always show temple, cheek, or jaw detail on a front view), you may have to arrange several mirrors in order to get a clear view. Or a good practice is to find someone who would be willing to do a profile drawing of you in exchange for your drawing one of him or her.

To make the process much simpler, lightly transfer the proportions in Figure 2–14 onto a large oval on your paper. These approximate those on the "average" head, so you can expect to have to make some modifications to suit the shape of your own face and placement of features.

Take special note of the width of your own face in proportion to the height, and lightly sketch the general shape of your head, including the jawline. Indicate with another light line where the

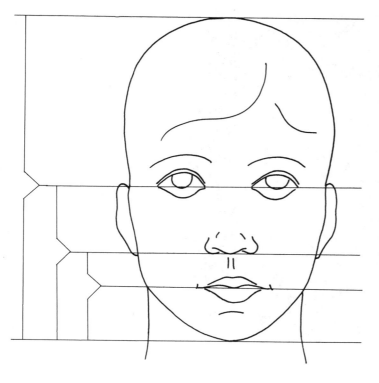

Figure 2–14.
Though every face differs in proportional relationships, this facial map, outlining the "average" features, is a good departure point when sketching realistic portraits.

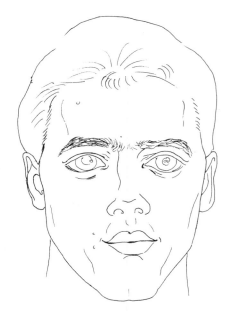

Figure 2–15.
Though contour drawings such
as this one are easier to do from
a photograph, drawing from
life will often yield more
information as to actual
three-dimensional form.

eyes fall on this shape—approximately halfway from the chin to the top of the head. The nostrils will be drawn in approximately halfway between this line and the chin, while the lip line appears a bit less than halfway between the nostril line and the chin. Now, before going any farther, check these indicators to your own features. A particularly long nose may necessitate dropping the nostril line or raising the eye line a bit. The average head is five "eyes" wide. The two eyes should be placed so that a third eye of equal size would fit between them. Leave room enough for another eye to fit between the outer corners and the sides of the head. Again, make adjustments that complement your own spacial relationships. Since the bridge of the nose is difficult to grasp with a line, concentrate on the nostrils and tip of the nose. Note the width of each by seeing where it lines up with the eye. Do the same with the lips. Generally, the outer edge of the mouth will fall directly beneath the very center of each eye. The ears should fit into the vertical space between the lip and eye lines.

Once this "map" has been sketched in lightly, step back from the drawing to get a different perspective. As any artist will confirm, we tend to become so involved with what we are creating that we often lose track of what is *really* happening on the paper. Either looking at it from a distance or going away and indulging in something else for a few moments will give you fresh insight. You may be able to solve easily the problem that had stumped you only minutes before. Whenever you are drawing—or applying makeup—take breaks every fifteen minutes or so. Remember too that most problems are not in the drawing, but in the seeing. So take time to study the subject matter with the eyes until the mind understands exactly what it is looking at.

Though all this drawing may seem tedious or frustrating to some, remember that these exercises are not meant to turn you into an easel artist. They are geared to learning elements that will be useful in thinking about character, exploring role-defined personality, and finding ways of expressing it. Sensitive performers or makeup artists need to develop a sensitivity to the faces they see daily, be able to pull information from them, find similarities and peculiarities, and have a useful means of recording that information and above all of expressing it. The magic of line provides just that avenue.

3

Form

A figure, barely more than a silhouette, shuffles painfully across the stage toward a singular spot of illumination. Trembling hands clutch a walking stick, its rigid symmetry a stark contrast to the bent, arthritic legs it supports. As the figure moves closer to the light, a shaggy white head tilts upwards, spilling the darkness from the face. An earnestly applied patchwork of highlight and shadow becomes immediate traitor to the blatant contours of youth, shattering in a second, the illusion of age so carefully conveyed by the actor's disciplined body.

Facial features, poorly conceived and created in haste or misunderstanding, can not only be distracting, but they can veritably destroy the believable visual communication that is so necessary between performer and audience.

Proper shading is the key to successful makeup application. With shadow and highlight, correctly applied, one can create the illusion of form where none exists and, to a large degree, eliminate certain features that aren't appropriate for a certain role.

33

Nearly everyone has known the tactile pleasure of running one's hand over a smooth sculpture, tracing with their fingers the silky undulations, gliding over a prominent feature and into a slippery furrow. One doesn't need to actually feel the sculpture to know its shape or the texture of its surface. The light shining on the object creates a pattern of shadows and highlights that instantly reveals this information to us.

Figures 3–1a and b show two simple pieces of paper. How differently they look. The light moving gradually over the surface in the first photograph "tells" us that the paper has been curved into a cylindrical shape. The sharp planes evidenced in the second photo inform us that the paper has been folded. The light changes as it collides with each fold, creating a shadowed area. The farther the crease is from the light source, the darker it appears.

Figure 3–1.

a   b

Figures 3–2a and b illustrate not only the contours of two different materials, but something of their texture as well. While the light slides relatively uninterrupted over the crumpled paper, tiny facets in the towel create a pattern of highlights and shadows that reveal the rough surface.

While the sculptor's efforts are revealed by the manner in which light caresses the sculpture, the easel artist must create the *illusion* of dimension on an otherwise flat canvas. Figure 3–2c is a charcoal sketch that, because of its patterns and placement of darks and lights, convinces us that we are looking at a three-dimensional form. The subtle movements from dark to light suggest that, like the paper cylinder and the towel, this is a soft, draped material rather than stiff paper or metal. The charcoal sketches in Figure 3–3 also give the impression of dimensional form—with the exception of the straight line in the lower left corner. Lacking shading, it remains static, without depth or dimension. (This will be important to remember when this chapter progresses into lines and wrinkles.) If you study these sketches, you will discover that the light areas

Figure 3–2.

a   b   c

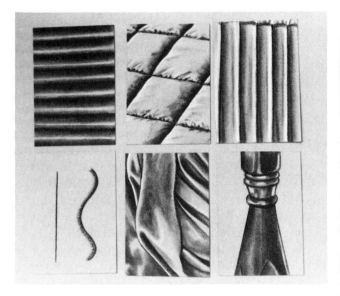

Figure 3–3.
Proper shading can create an unlimited
array of illusions.

seem to advance toward the eye, while the darker areas seem to recede, creating a movement from one area to the next. The eye does, in fact, interpret light areas as being closer and larger than dark areas of identical size. The lighter an area, the closer it appears. The darker, the deeper it seems to be.

This principle provides the foundation for all makeup: *Lights advance; darks recede.* By adhering to this rule, a skilled makeup artist can "lengthen" a chin, "flatten" a nose, "broaden" a jaw, or "heighten" a forehead. In fact, there is little short of violating natural proportions that a makeup artist *can't* do to alter the very structure of a performer's face.

Figures 3–4a through c illustrate just how powerful the light-dark principle is. This young actress, working from an ink sketch, altered the shape of her entire face using just white and black. The eye accepts this new structure, even in this stylized, almost cartoon style. Note how a new ear and nose have been created by the placement of the darks and lights. The eye tends to almost eliminate the portions of the ear that have been blackened, while acknowledging the new bulbous nose created by the white.

Obviously, shapes and lines done in black and white can create illusions. Such a stylized approach, however, is rarely appropriate on the stage.

36

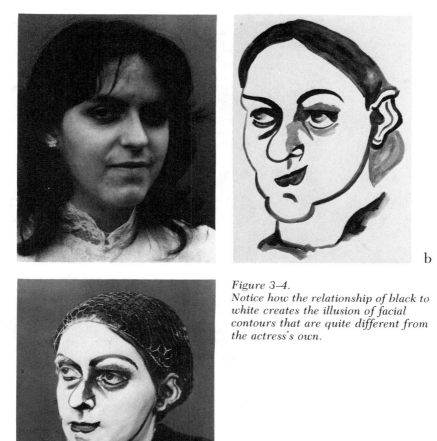

a

b

c

Figure 3–4.
Notice how the relationship of black to white creates the illusion of facial contours that are quite different from the actress's own.

The same visual impact can be created to a more realistic end using the same principle of lights versus darks, as illustrated in Figure 3–5. Because of the large light area between the eyes, the viewer gravitates there, thus making them seem farther apart. By placing the lights at the outside corners of the eyes, as has been done in the bottom example, the viewer focuses outward, "pushing" the eyes closer together.

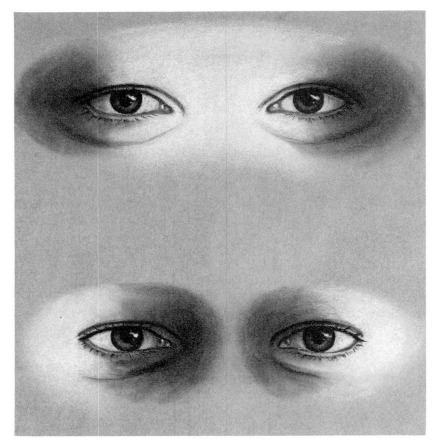

Figure 3–5.
Very realistic illusions can be created by manipulating lights and darks. These eyes are identical in size and distance apart.

Another realistic example of using lights and darks to alter structure is shown in Figures 3–6a and b. This actress seems to have changed the very shape of her jaw. The lighter color was applied to create the desired shape, while the darks work to emphasize and sharpen the illusion.

Believable contours do not happen by accident, of course. Like all artists, those doing makeup must lay out their ideas on paper first, working out the problems and finalizing their solutions. Developing shading skills is vital in applying makeup. Understanding the application begins by sketching.

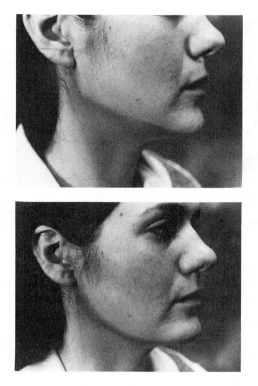

Figure 3–6.

The human face is composed of various shapes—a cone for the bridge of the nose, a sphere for the nostrils and eyes, a cylinder for the forehead, and so on. Rendering basic forms is therefore an important first step. Cut shapes out of styrofoam or gather such objects as a box, ball, soup can, or cone that approximate the basic geometric shapes. Place the objects on a flat surface with directional lighting coming from one side. Do your rendering on a sheet of colored construction paper so that you can include the highlights, using chalk or a white charcoal pencil. Always start with the lightest areas first. Then, with your finger or a charcoal stump, blend them into the darks. Your drawing might look like Figures 3–7a or b. If the blending is not smooth, it might appear like Figure 3–7c. Learn to blend well on paper, for if skills are not learned and applied to the face, ragged blending will appear as blotches or smudges on the human features. The illusion of form and contour is consequently destroyed, as a well intentioned cheek hollow may very well read like a large, ugly dent!

a

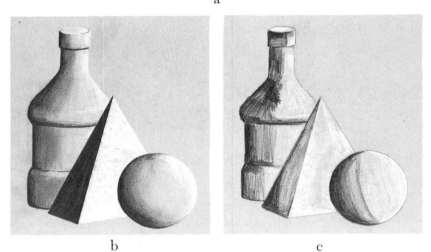

b   c

Figure 3–7.
Shading objects composed of the basic shapes is excellent practice for creating
form where none exists on the human face.

Try to get the darkest darks you can from the pencil or charcoal, as well as the whitest whites for maximum contrast. Figures
3–8a and b illustrate well the difference between a ho-hum low-
contrast makeup, and one that creates distinct form. Though one
may not want great contrast for a youthful character, it is necessary
when modeling old age or when creating other drastic structural
changes for an ordinary playing distance.

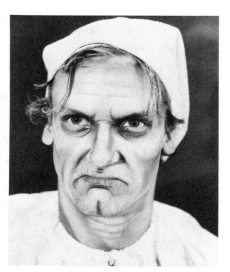

a

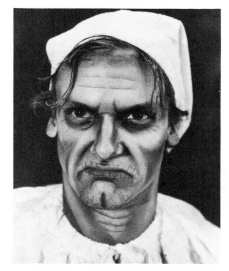

b

Figure 3–8.
Underexposing one of these
photographs shows clearly that
contrast is a vital concern in
applying makeup. Figure 3–8a is
weak and would fail to read at a
great audience distance, while
3–8b would carry effectively.

The next step is to apply these shading principles to the human face. You might begin by actually copying black-and-white photographs to see how light plays over each feature. If a photo has a large hooked nose, notice how the light and dark patterns reveal it. Note how the lights and darks combine to create large bags beneath the eyes. Such lessons can be applied almost directly to the human face.

a

Figure 3–9.
One can easily translate light and dark patterns from a photograph in determining how each works to create form. Analyze each feature and then carefully duplicate the picture, seeing if you can create the same facial forms.

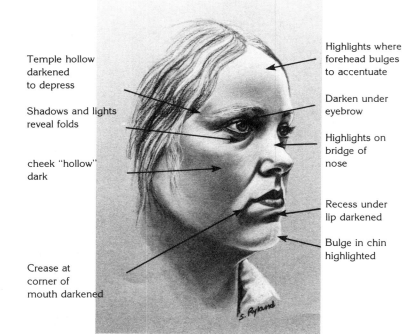

Temple hollow
darkened
to depress

Shadows and lights
reveal folds

cheek "hollow"
dark

Crease at
corner of
mouth darkened

Highlights where
forehead bulges
to accentuate

Darken under
eyebrow

Highlights on
bridge of
nose

Recess under
lip darkened

Bulge in chin
highlighted

b

As you draw each picture, try to imagine that it is somehow inflatable. If expanded to its actual three-dimensional form, what would it feel like to a blind person? Would the chin be round and smooth to the touch, or rough and angular? Would the eyes drop back into their sockets, or would they be obscured by sagging eyelids? Imagine each protruding area as being light in color, gradually fading into darkness as it moves into a natural depression.

Exploring the Human Face

The makeup artist is suspended somewhere between the easel artist, who works on a flat surface, and the sculptor, who works with actual form. It would be quite simple to alter the structure, texture, and overall shape of the human face if in fact it were as flat as a chalkboard. One could simply erase and add new features at whim! Our own faces, however, have a dimension of their own; this dimension varies from person to person and from year to year during the course of one's lifetime. To fully comprehend the human face, and thus to be able to alter it, one must comprehend it as a sculptural piece.

Getting a "feel" of the features will enable you to recreate them more easily. In addition, it will help you to understand the limitations imposed by anatomical structure. One person's jaw may lend itself very well to pouchy jowels, while trying to create this illusion on someone with a sharp jutting jawline might be disastrous.

Drawing faces is, of course, helpful, but not before actually exploring each of the features and noting how they relate. Close your eyes to eliminate any distractions. Start with the fingers of both hands back to back at the vertical center of the forehead. Slowly pull the fingers toward the ears on either side. Mentally note any undulations beneath your fingertips.

Some people have a prominent ridge on which the eyebrows ride, while others have a peak in the middle. Others are perfectly flat like the side of a box. What happens as you reach the outer edge? Is there a rigid edge over which your fingers fall into the temple area, or a gradual smooth curve into this space? (How would you shade a portrait to achieve this edge?) Note the soft depression of the temple.

Gently determine the perimeters of this depression, and then progress downward to the cheek bones. Are they high and obvious, or low on the face and flat? Find the point at which they project away from the skull the most and follow this edge to the nose, feeling with your fingers how it connects to this feature. Note that if you follow the bone of the nose upward, it circles around the eye, forming the bony cavity that houses our organs of vision. Depending on the structure of this opening and the amount of flesh over and under the eye, aging might cause the eye to sink back into this socket, forming a depression. Other people form large baggy areas around the eye. Can you determine how your own flesh will fall in old age within this area?

Return to the bridge of the nose. Find the edge at which the skull ends and the cartilage forming the lower half of the nose begins. Carefully explore the three bulbs that compose the end of your nose and nostrils. As you touch your nose, note its full contour. Is it long and sharp on the bridge, or perhaps flat and rounded at the bottom?

Return your fingers to the cheek bones and pull downward. As you age, flesh will begin to droop from taut cheeks onto the soft, unsupported area beneath. This cheek "hollow" is often accentuated with makeup. As you move toward the jawline, one of several things may happen. Some people have tightly drawn cheeks that keep the skin pulled taut over the jaw. Others may have a great deal of loose flesh covering the entire cheek area, perhaps even continuing into a double chin under the jaw. Many people have a slight indentation, which then rounds out into a soft fullness that "pads" the jawline. If many teeth are missing, a definite hollowness may be perceived. Let your fingers follow the length of your jaw. Where does it begin? Is it symmetrical? (Many aren't!) Is it well padded or in sharp contrast to the neck?

Return the fingers to the cheek and move toward the center of your face while smiling broadly, so as to create a distinct nasalabial fold. Some ridges are soft, falling onto the jawline, while others are full and high on the face. Follow your own, finding the area of greatest fullness. If you feel carefully, you will find that the space between the nose and top lip swells in the center from a low point in the nasalabial furrow. It also stands out farther where it meets the actual lip than it does where it connects to the base of the nostrils. If you were emphasizing this area with darks and lights, where might you utilize each in adhering to the natural form?

Midway across this portion of the face lies the philtrum, a vertical dent that extends from just under the nose to the top lip. The lips themselves also emanate from a low area in the nasalabial furrow. Run your finger from corner to corner, feeling the sense of cylindrical roundness. Then run your fingers from just under your nose to your chin, sensing every undulation. The top lip rounds into the lip line and swells out again to accommodate the bottom member. An indentation immediately under the lip then eases into a swelling that is the chin. Explore the chin a moment to see if it is essentially a small round ball—or flat, square, sharp, or padded.

Once you have taken this journey with your eyes closed, find a mirror and repeat the exercise with both your fingers and your eyes. As you move over prominent areas such as the cheek bones or bridge of the nose, try to imagine them in light chalk, gradually becoming a dark charcoal as you move into recessions. Pretend you are creating this sense of form on flat paper; then do just that. As you attempt this self-portrait, use no lines, but rely on only your lights and darks to capture the shape of your nose, cheeks, and lips. Use your first self-portrait only as a guide for placement of features.

Figure 3–10.
This self portrait employs shading to create dimensional cheeks and nose.

Sculpting a likeness of yourself in clay can be an effective bridge between sketching and actually solving dimensional problems on your face. About eight pounds of plasticine or other oil-based clay is needed to do a life-sized face. With this very flexible model, you can easily alter facial features. By then observing how light plays over the surface, you can learn how to recreate that particular feature on the face.

Reshaping the Nose

Figures 3–11a and b show how easily one may change the shape of a nose by simply giving it a push one way or the other. Figures 3–12a, b, and c are sketches done by observing the light patterns on three different configurations of the clay nose. Refer to Figures 3–12d, e, and f to see just how these applications worked on a real face.

Figure 3–11.
A flexible clay face is wonderful for exploring form.

a   b

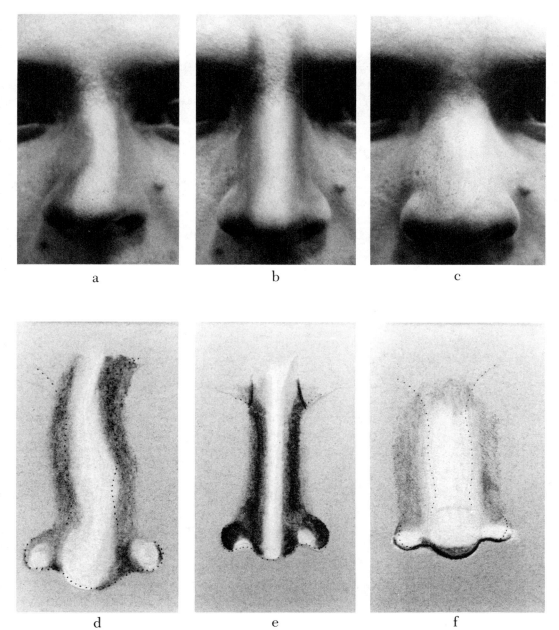

a   b   c

d   e   f

Figure 3–12.

Since the nose can be a fun feature to work with, let's graduate to actually applying makeup and give ourselves a new look! The principles of light-dark will stay essentially the same. The areas that we want to be prominent will be rendered in light makeup, while a darker color will serve as the negative area, or as a support system for the lights. Remember that the human eye tends to ignore the dark areas.

Since we are simply trying to create an effect, practice blending, and get used to working with pigment on actual complexions, the colors are not particularly important. White, with just a touch of yellow or red to temper its starkness will be fine for the highlights, while a dark color such as a blue or brown will be fine for the shading (see Chapter 6). Cream liners are suggested for this exercise since they will be utilized exclusively in the color sections of this book. Now is an excellent opportunity to become familiar with them.

Cream liners come in circular plastic containers of less than one ounce each. Though this may seem like a miniscule amount, only a tiny bit is used for an actual makeup project, and one container will easily last through the run of several productions. When working with colored liners, one must think of a scenic or artist's canvas. The raw material has a good deal of texture that is obliterated when layers of paint are applied. When one dyes that same piece of fabric, color is attained without sacrificing the fresh quality of a textural surface. Think of your face as that piece of fabric. The greatest single mistake made by people who apply makeup is that they put on too much. Makeup on television looks very natural because almost no makeup is used. Remember this and keep it thin!

Simply wipe a finger across the surface of the white cosmetic liner, taking just enough to color the finger. Then put it into the palm of your opposite hand, which will serve as a palette for mixing colors. Because colors and brands of cream liners may differ in consistency, the heat of the palm serves to aid in blending them smoothly. Mixing colors on the hand provides a sure test of how they will look on the complexion. Also, the hand can be held next to the face in the mirror to determine how each newly mixed color will "work" with those already on the face.

a

b

c

Figure 3–13.
In three easy steps, you can completely
alter the shape of your nose.

To this smear of white, add a tiny bit of yellow or red liner, blending the two. Then pull the finger along the bridge of the nose (as shown in Figure 3–14), establishing a "crook." Using a clean finger, blend the edges softly into the adjacent complexion. If you end up rubbing too much makeup off, destroying the illusion of advancement, simply apply more. Practice will teach you the proper amount.

When the light color is properly placed, put a smear of the dark color on a clean portion of your palm. (Taking color directly from the container can lead to gobbing and placement mistakes.)

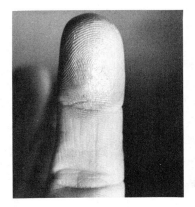

Figure 3–14.
Very little makeup is necessary to create
illusions.

Figure 3–14 shows the proper amount, which, as you can see, hardly fills in the natural crevices on the finger. Place this dark color on either side of the light area and gently "tap" the darker color into the light, coaxing it to blend smoothly. Do the same with the outer edges.

Step back to evaluate the effect from the distance. Have you applied the makeup so heavily that your nose reads like the prow of a ship? Is the blending smooth where lights meet darks? Does it read well, or does it fade into the natural complexion? Answer these questions and make adjustments. If you are pleased, wipe off the crooked illusion and try the others in Figures 3–12b and c.

The Thick-Thin Exercise

The following exercise will not only test your comprehension of the light-dark theory and shading skills, it will provide you with knowledge that is directly applicable to almost every makeup project you may encounter.

Study the facial maps in Figures 3–15a and b. One has utilized the lights to emphasize the vertical aspects of the face, thus making it look longer and leaner, while the other has minimized these areas with darks and used the lights to make the horizontal features look more prominent. Note, for instance, how lights have been pulled up into the hairline, as well as under the nose and chin, to force the eye to stretch the full length of the face on Figure 3–15b.

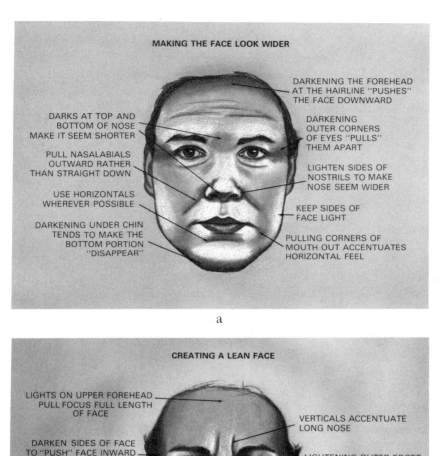

MAKING THE FACE LOOK WIDER

DARKENING THE FOREHEAD AT THE HAIRLINE "PUSHES" THE FACE DOWNWARD

DARKS AT TOP AND BOTTOM OF NOSE MAKE IT SEEM SHORTER

PULL NASALABIALS OUTWARD RATHER THAN STRAIGHT DOWN

USE HORIZONTALS WHEREVER POSSIBLE

DARKENING UNDER CHIN TENDS TO MAKE THE BOTTOM PORTION "DISAPPEAR"

DARKENING OUTER CORNERS OF EYES "PULLS" THEM APART

LIGHTEN SIDES OF NOSTRILS TO MAKE NOSE SEEM WIDER

KEEP SIDES OF FACE LIGHT

PULLING CORNERS OF MOUTH OUT ACCENTUATES HORIZONTAL FEEL

a

CREATING A LEAN FACE

LIGHTS ON UPPER FOREHEAD PULL FOCUS FULL LENGTH OF FACE

DARKEN SIDES OF FACE TO "PUSH" FACE INWARD

LIGHTEN VERTICAL CENTER OF NOSE

LIGHTEN CHIN TO PULL FOCUS DOWNWARD

VERTICALS ACCENTUATE LONG NOSE

LIGHTENING OUTER EDGES OF EYES "PUSHES" THEM CLOSER TOGETHER

DARKEN THE NOSTRILS SO THAT BRIDGE WILL HAVE FOCUS

PULL NASALABIALS AND CORNERS OF MOUTH DOWNWARD

b

Figure 3–15.

In addition, the sides of the face have been "pushed in" by using darks. The opposite is true on Figure 3–15a. Transfer the areas of these maps *lightly* with a maroon eyebrow pencil to the face. Place the thin map on one half of the face, while attempting the wider look on the other. Because it is important to step back and gauge the process, it might be wise to find a "volunteer" for this project.

Begin again with a yellow-white or red-white mixture, and apply it to all of the areas on both sides of the face that are prominent. Place the smear of light color in the center of each area and blend outward, rather than filling each in like a paint-by-number

Figure 3–16.
The top row of this series indicates placement of lights and darks to create a sensation of thinness as well as weightiness. The bottom row shows how each side should look once it is blended.

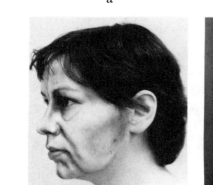

a

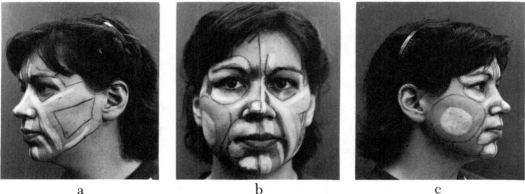

b

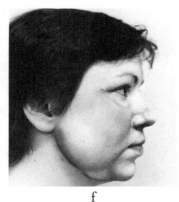

c

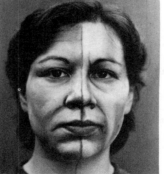

d

e

f

painting. Step back to evaluate whether some areas may need a little more of the white mixture to "pump them up" a bit. Next apply a smear of the dark color to the center of each area that is designated to recede. With a clean finger, pull the color outwards, again gently "tapping" to blend the edge into the light areas. You may have to add a bit more dark to those areas that demand a greater sense of depth.

Finishing touches can be added with a quarter-inch brush to complete the illusion. On the heavier side, extend the lip line outward just a bit, while pulling it straight down on the thin side. Do the same with the eyes. Emphasizing the nasalabial or adding a vertical cleft would help on the long lean side as well. Wrinkles on the forehead will add to the horizontal illusion on the heavier side, while emphasizing the drooping bag beneath the eyes on the lean side will accentuate the long look.

A brush becomes a necessity when working with delicate features, because the fingers are too large and clumsy for details. Figure 3–17 shows an actress creating the illusion of forehead

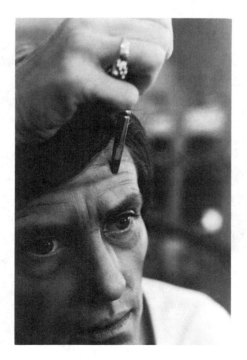

Figure 3–17.
Feathering in shadows can create not only the deep portion of a wrinkle, but a sense of protruding form as well.

wrinkles by using a flat ferrule brush, the most useful type in sculpting form. The thin edge of the brush is used to carefully define the very center of each fold or wrinkle, as shown in Figure 3–18a. Left as such, however, a line remains without dimension (like the square in Figure 3–18b), a simple "cut" on the face. The flat edge of the brush is then used for gently and evenly pulling the color outward toward the adjacent light area and blending the two. Sometimes, when one desires a very deep fold, this line must be applied and brushed outward several times to build up a convincing movement from light to dark. Remember, to be convincing, the transition must not be abrupt, but flow gently, as light does around a cylinder. Try experimenting with a brush to create folds and wrinkles before moving on to the final projects in this chapter.

Figure 3–18.

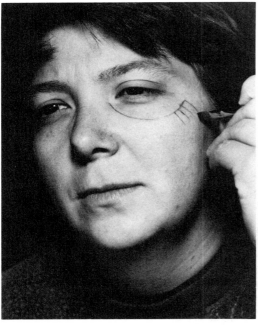

a

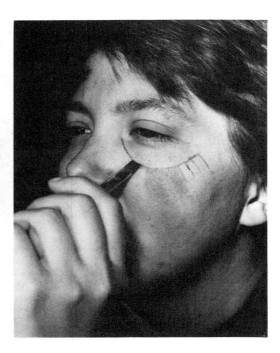

b

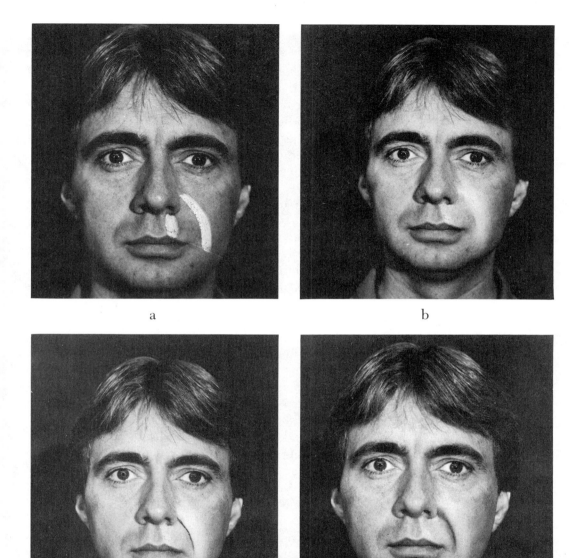

a b

c d

Figure 3–19.
Always remember to establish the lightest areas before adding the darker colors for the maximum effect.

The most common problem facing the young actor is age, which requires a great deal of analysis and skill to render convincingly. The results often look painted and phony. This is generally due to one of two factors: Either the performer is not thoroughly acquainted with his or her own facial features and how they will naturally age, or the sequence of application finds the young performer applying wrinkles before a convincing, sculptural "base" has been established.

One must adhere to one's own anatomy when attempting two-dimensional old age. One cannot create massive sagging jowels on a sharp jawline without having the shadows created by the lighting reveal the true facial structure. By the same token, vertical creases and wrinkles cannot be rendered where naturally horizontal folds lie. The actress in Figure 3–20a spent considerable time exploring her own face to determine what would happen as she aged. She also consulted photos of her grandparents as well as magazine pictures for "appropriate" structures. The resulting makeup in Figure 3–20b reflects this study. Figures 6–6a through 6–6n (Chapter 6) show a step-by-step application of old age makeup that results in quite a different division of features, as determined by that particular actress's face. Compare the step in Figure 3–20c with that shown in Figure 3–20b. Note, for instance, how differently the cheeks, nasalabials, and foreheads are treated. Though both applications work well on the facial structure to which they are applied, neither would "play" well on the other actress as she moved and spoke under theatrical lights, since the natural contours and expressions would "fight" with those created with makeup.

Many performers simply rely on the application of wrinkles to lend a sense of age, a move that often reads like a busy road map or simply as dirt at a distance. Creating believable old age relies on color, texture, and most of all a carefully formed contour of sagging soft flesh. Without this initial shaping of the face, wrinkles and details will simply not be convincing.

After studying your own face and consulting many pictures of old people, try drawing a picture of yourself as you might look fifty

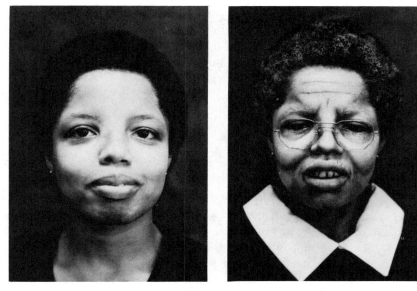

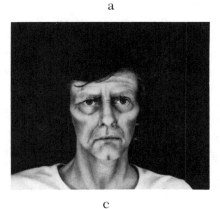

Figure 3–20.
Just as each of us age to look quite different, old age makeup must reflect that individuality.

years from now. Remember to use dark darks and light lights, as maximum contrast is usually needed to successfully convey the exaggerated dimension of deep nasalabial folds and sagging jowels or eye bags. Try to avoid the use of wrinkles, concentrating on the overall movement of the flesh defining each feature. When you are pleased with your comprehension and solutions, transfer the sketch to your face, beginning again with the lightest, most prominent areas. Step back from the mirror as far as possible to determine whether or not the lights are in the correct places, and whether they do, in fact, carry the illusion. If you are not pleased, they may need more "beefing up" or a bit of altering in placement. If you are pleased, continue with the darks, reinforcing the lights in carving out bags and folds.

Developing a Likeness

The ultimate test of one's manipulative skills with light and shadow illusion comes when one must duplicate the features of another person on his or her own face. This task demands that performers not only know their own faces very well, but analyze with scrutiny the face of the person to be duplicated to locate every similarity and difference. Some features on the performer must be seemingly enlargened, lengthened, or otherwise accented, while some (perhaps inappropriate ones) must be subdued or eliminated altogether. The actor in Figure 3–21a was asked to portray a long-deceased dignitary, whose photo appears in Figure 3–21b. As you can see, the historical figure possessed a wider jaw, more prominent nasalabials, heavier eyelids, a rounder larger nose, and, of course, considerably different hair. Because the audience was to be exceptionally close, great exaggerations were out of the question. Over a tracing of his own photograph, the actor worked with pencil and chalk to determine the changes that could logically be made without the use of three-dimensional prosthetics. As you can see, the finished makeup does indeed transform the actor into the man from another century.

While Chapter 1 focused on design preparation, this chapter concentrated on expanding that preparation into a very realistic dimensional form. Color, the ultimate design tool, is covered in the following chapters. With it the makeup artist can not only create all the effects and illusions obtained with black and white, but produce an endless repertoire of facial complexions. Color is the medium that adds life to the sketch on the portrait painter's canvas and to the actor's face on stage.

a

b

c

d

Figure 3–21.

4

Color Basics

Color
as Paradox

No other medium than color has so intrigued and captured the human imagination. No sensation affects us in so many ways, adding richness and meaning to our lives. The human conception of color has permeated the realms of mysticism, sorcery, alchemy, religion, philosophy, medicine, psychology, and, almost incidentally, art.

To the ancient and not so ancient world, color was purely symbolic in nature. The color of an object determined its magical powers over the elements. The Greeks used raven eggs to restore the blackness to graying hair. Centuries later, the English gobbled down spiders rolled in butter to cure yellow jaundice on the premise that the color of the disease required a cure of the same hue. The French believed that wrapping in red blankets would ward off smallpox's crimson sores. As recently as a century ago, doctors diagnosed colored cures for any malady. Many a citizen walked the streets with his temples painted blue to ward off a headache.

It was not, in fact, until the Renaissance that humankind even began to think of color in aesthetic forms, and only in the last century have people truly explored its artistic magic. Studies have shown the powerful effect that color has on our moods, tastes, biases, and habits. Artists, interior decorators, architects, and scenic designers have incorporated these predictable human responses into their creations, successfully manipulating our very environments. Painters employ a rich variety of hues in such a way as to evoke a response from the viewer, whether the canvas speaks in one color or as a lush merger of dozens of hues. There are no artists in fact—be they potters, weavers, or makeup artists—who can *avoid* using color. It therefore only makes sense that makeup artists learn all they can about this magical medium and use it to full advantage.

Makeup is sadly trailing behind the other arts in its employment of color. The potential has not only been neglected, but often blatantly misused, resulting in makeup that frequently appears lifeless and fake. By understanding just how the eye perceives color and by utilizing painting methods that add life to a canvas, the makeup artist can produce a sense of vibrancy and believability that is unattainable with conventional methods of application.

Color is a curious paradox in that there are actually two separate color systems existing in our everyday world. The first and most familiar is taught to most of us somewhere in our educational journey. This system explains color relationships in pigments—pastels, paints, crayons, and the like. As the standard color wheel (Plate 11 in the color section) illustrates, there is a predictability in terms of color blending. Red mixed with yellow, for instance, will always produce an orange color.

The second color system is less familiar, and it may therefore seem more abstract. This system operates on scientific principles that explain *why* we (think we) see any given color(s). Allowing a ray of sunlight to pass through a prism will help explain this theory more clearly.

Color exists only in light. We actually live not in a world of colored objects, but in a world of colorless surfaces that reflect back a particular length of light wave, which our eyes interpret as a color. When one looks at a can of yellow paint, one is seeing only the yellow rays reflected back. The remainder of the colored rays are absorbed. When we replace the lid on that can of paint, there is, in fact, no color inside!

It is not important to understand all the "whys" concerning this physical fact. What is important to remember is that, although the yellow is predominant, the other colors are in fact present. Materials all respond to light differently. Some, like velvet or a flower petal, allow colors to penetrate deeply, causing a rich sense of coloration that seems to vibrate when placed next to a piece of construction paper of the same hue. Other materials, such as metals, have a surface that causes the light rays to bounce back, creating white highlights.

Color and Art

No object in nature is the one-dimensional static color we assume it to be. This implies a tremendous difference between what our eyes actually take in and what our minds convince us we are seeing. The artist must bridge that inconsistency in order to duplicate nature with all its internal color-cueing. Anyone can learn to see color in all its splendor. One must simply unlearn years of limited conditioning.

Color assignment begins when we are children, eagerly grasping our crayolas in tiny fists obliterating the white sterile pages of our coloring books. Apples are red. Donkeys are brown. Leaves are green. At no time were we encouraged to advance beyond that stage of conscious color processing. In fact, we were probably discouraged from using any color except the "appropriate" one. Thus, we learned to see in "object color." Neither education nor experience has taught most of us to see internal color. Consequently, we are only vaguely aware of it—and then only when the richness in color is *missing*, thus denying the eye the color cues necessary to convince our minds that the object is real. We do not, for instance, believe that an apple painted in flat red is real. Most plastic flowers and fruit, rendered in a single shade of yellow or green, look fake.

Correspondingly, we can immediately tell when someone has on a layer of makeup or has dyed hair. *Why?* The eye needs lots of colors to register "real." The eye finds a flat area of any given color boring and tiresome. By painting a portrait with a palette rich in colors—blues, purples, oranges, and greens—the resulting "flesh" tone looks real. The same remedy is necessary to give life to a performer wearing makeup . . . color.

Plate 1 is an example of "primitive" art. Artists who paint in this style adhere to "object" color. The results seem flat, like a layer of greasepaint. Plate 2 is an example of a portrait done in color. Notice the difference between the two. Now look at Plates 4 and 5. Can you tell which side was done with pancake and which was done with color? The approach with color provides complexion and structural features simultaneously, while the pancake tends to obliterate both.

Capturing the color sensation is not limited to paint and canvas, or to makeup. Refer to Plates 9 and 10. Every picture, whether it be in a book or on television, is actually a composite of many colors, which blend to give us a singular sensation. One can explore this phenomenon further by looking at a newspaper or magazine with a magnifying glass. You may be surprised at the colors necessary to give the impression of black, green, or white.

This illusion was first explored by the late nineteenth-century school of painters known as the Impressionists. Manet, Renoir, and their contemporaries become intrigued with the scientific experiments with color of their day. These experiments seemed to indicate that, for the first fraction of a second that the eye focuses on anything, it actually receives the impression of all colors present. In striving to capture that moment on canvas, they abandoned object color entirely and utilized a full spectrum. Their paintings were composed of tiny bits of color, which at close range look like only a random profusion of dots. When the viewer steps back, however, the eye fuses the dots into a lively and realistic painting of the subject matter. Plate 8 shows a painting done in this style.

Color in makeup is certainly not applied in dots, but it may be obvious when viewed at mirror-range. However, like the painting, one needs only to step back a few feet, and the face will melt into a rich, believable complexion.

Until now, only portrait artists have utilized color in creating complexion. Most makeup artists, lacking the background in color usage, tend to use it on the lips, cheeks, or eyes. Only when the opportunity arises to create a fantasy character do they venture into the spectral world of color possibilities.

The following chapter expands on color perception and usage, explaining how only three colors (red, yellow, and blue) can compose an entire makeup kit! Understanding the color concept enables one to abandon greasepaints and pancakes entirely and to apply makeup in a new, more realistic way. Working from a palette of color is a lot of fun, though admittedly a challenge at first. The rewards, however, are exciting. Whether you decide to adopt the color theory in its entirety or simply integrate it with approaches you are more familiar with, just understanding how color can improve makeup is a valuable step in daring to utilize it.

5

Color Terminology

**The Mechanics
of Color**

Applying straight colors to the face may seem a bit foreign to those who are used to working with pancake and greasepaint. Once an understanding of color is established, however, the process seems quite simple and really a lot of fun.

This chapter on color terminology may be simply a refresher for some, while the vocabulary will be quite new for others. Yet taking time to learn it will, like a verbal vocabulary, provide an endless means of expression.

Color has three basic properties, or ways in which it can be described: its *position* on the color wheel, its *value*, and its *intensity*. Each is an important variable in talking about and in understanding how color works.

Position on the Color Wheel. The color wheel shown in Plate 11 and Figure 5–1 shows the relationship between all of the colors. Yellow, red, and blue are known as the three *primary* colors. All of the colors in our world are combinations of just these three!

The three *secondary* colors—green, purple, and orange—are achieved by mixing equal amounts of the primary colors that lie on

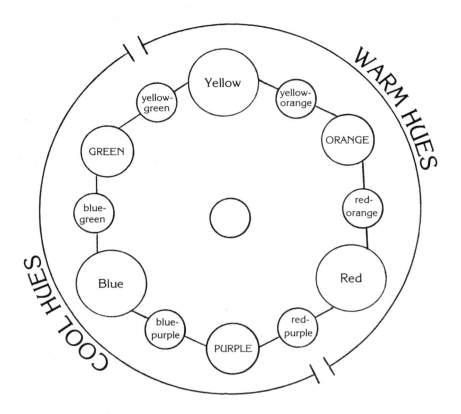

Figure 5–1.
This color wheel and the one in Plate 11 illustrate how each color relates to the other when mixing paints or makeup.

either side of them. Red and yellow, for instance, combine to produce orange.

The hundreds of thousands of remaining colors in the world are known as *tertiary* colors. Each is a product of mixing two primaries together in unequal portions. Such colors include red-oranges, yellow-greens, and the like.

Browns are unique in that they are created by mixing all three of the primaries together. A reddish-brown such as sienna obviously has more red in proportion to blue or yellow, while an ochre-brown would have an abundance of yellow.

Making one's own color wheel is the best way to develop color-mixing skills as well as to grasp a firm understanding of color relationships. One needs only the three primary colors found in a basic watercolor set.

After allowing a few drops of water to soften the blocks of colors, transfer several brushloads of yellow to the lid of the watercolor box or to a small plate. You will need a puddle about the size of a silver dollar. On a sheet of fairly heavy paper, paint a square of pure yellow. Then, with the tip of a clean brush, transfer a *tiny* drop of red to the yellow puddle and mix. Place a swatch of the resulting color next to the first yellow square. Continue adding one drop of red at a time and recording the resulting colors until the puddle and the swatch have turned pure red. You may very well have some enormous "skips" between colors—where too much or too little red was added. Simply cut out the ones that best represent a smooth gradation from yellow through orange to red, and paste them onto a clean sheet of paper. Complete the color wheel by adding blue to yellow and blue to red. Trying to work the darker color to the lighter demands an enormous amount of paint and time.

Figure 5–2.
Though a simple set of water colors is all that is necessary to make one's own color scales, acrylics, tube water colors, or even oil paints may be utilized!

Figure 5–3.

Once your color wheel is complete, try to determine where various objects around you might fall on the spectrum. Would that green couch, for instance, fall closer to yellow or to blue? Is a blue dress actually a primary, or does it have a hint of purple to it?

Note that half of the color wheel in Figure 5–1 is labeled "cool" and half is labeled "warm." Warm colors are reminiscent of the sun or fire . . . friendly, exciting elements. Greens, blues, and purples are perceived as being more subdued and relaxing. The important thing to remember about warm and cool colors is that they can be used to create contrast and dimension. In the chapter on shading, darks were used to create the impression of receding. Cool colors provide this same illusion, while warm colors, like highlights, seem to advance toward the eye.

Value.   Black and white are not included on the color wheel, since they are not created by the primaries. Both are essential, however, in creating the *value* of any color. Color Plate 12 illustrates how a color can be lowered in value by adding black, creating a *shade* of that color. Adding white to a color raises the value to a *tint*. Often, tints of a color are referred to as "pastels."

Note that tints advance, while shades, being darker, recede. Even a blue, which is normally a cool, receding color, can be made to come forward by adding white. Yet a warm, prominent orange can become a receding color simply by adding black. (See Plate 14 in the color section.) The basic principle of creating dimension— "lights advance, darks recede"—still applies. The "lights" have simply been expanded to include warm colors and tints of any color, while "darks" include cool colors and shades of any color.

It may help to "set" the idea of a value in your mind by making a value scale. One needs only add black progressively to a puddle of color for shades. To raise the value, add either white or clear water, which allows the white of the paper to make the color appear lighter.

As you observe the completed value scale, note that the color with the greatest proportion of white seems to stand out the most, while the darkest colors seem to fade back into the paper. Apply the lessons learned in shading to this color scale, remembering that the greatest contrast is achieved by using the two extremes. On a very old face one might have to utilize both ends of the value scale to effectively create deep bags and wrinkles. On a youthful face, colors in the middle ranges are probably more appropriate. (Note Plate 16.)

Again, check your comprehension of value by placing objects around you on a value scale. Is the automobile a primary red, or is it a tint or shade? Are the leaves on one tree a higher tint than on another? Which of five orange books is lowest on the value scale?

Intensity. The *intensity* of a color is sometimes confused with value. The intensity of a color is its *brightness* (or lack thereof). When the intensity of colors used on the face, in a costume, or on the scenery is all the same, a pleasing picture has been created. If one color is much brighter, it will draw focus from the others. Sometimes this emphasis is desirable, but more often it is not. Balancing the intensities (see Plate 15) of all the colors used in a makeup is important, or your efforts will all look clownish!

One can both lower the intensity of a color and fool the eye into thinking you have raised it by using the color's *complement*.

Complements are colors that lie directly across from one another on the color wheel. The Christmas colors of red and green are complements, as are the choices for Easter, purple and yellow.

As you can see in Plate 13, adding one complement to the other diminishes their brightness. Red can be dulled down to a boring gray-brown by adding a considerable amount of green, and vice versa. There is no way to actually make any given color more intense, but one can make it "seem" brighter by placing its complement *beside* it. This trick provided the backbone of the op art movement of the sixties. By placing stripes or shapes of bright complementary colors next to one another, each seemed to vibrate with life . . . so much so, in fact, that one could not look at the canvas for long without risking a headache! Scenic painters utilize this trick when they spatter green foliage with bright red to add a visual punch. One may do the same thing in makeup by stippling a bland application of Oriental yellow with bright purple. From a short distance, the complementary accents disappear, leaving only a lively look to the base colors.

Again, making an intensity scale with your watercolors is an important step in understanding how intensity differs from value, as well as how they can be utilized in makeup. Begin with a puddle of the warmest color and add drops of that color's complement to progressively complete a full scale.

Return to the objects you identified on the value scale and try to determine their intensities. Two objects, such as a "happy face" sticker and a legal yellow pad, may both be high on a yellow value scale, yet one is certainly duller than the other and thus lower on the intensity scale. See if you can clarify subtle differences.

Grasping color terminology will certainly help in defining the kaleidoscope of color that surrounds us and in applying it to makeup for the human face. The following chapter incorporates all this knowledge in explaining an innovative approach to makeup using only pure color.

Analogous Colors. Analogous colors lie next to one another on the color wheel, but they encompass no more than one-third of the circle.

Complements. Complementary colors lie directly across from one another on the color wheel.

Cool. The half of the color wheel containing blue-purples, blues, blue-greens, and greens is known as the "cool half." These colors tend to elicit a relaxed response in the viewer, and they can actually lower blood pressure because of their calming effect.

Hue. "Hue" and "color" may be used interchangeably, as both denote a particular point on the color spectrum.

Intensity. The intensity of a color is its brightness. A low intensity hue is one that is grayed in coloration.

Monochromatic. This color scheme employs only one color, deriving variation through the addition of black or white.

Pigment. Any colored media, be it paint or makeup, is known as a pigment.

Primary. The primary colors are yellow, red, and blue. These colors cannot be created by mixing any other colors together. When combined with one another, however, they produce an endless array of different hues.

Secondary. Orange, green, and purple are secondary colors. Each is created by mixing equal proportions of two primaries.

Shade. A particular shade of any color can be created by adding black to it. Maroon is a shade of red.

Spectrum. All of the colors present in light as it spills through a prism are included in the spectrum. This full range of colors has been arranged into a color wheel to illustrate color relationships.

Tertiary. Intermediate colors, or all those not included as primary or secondary, are known as tertiary hues.

Triad. A triad is a combination of any three colors that lie equally distant from one another on the color wheel.

Value. One raises the value of a color by adding white, while the addition of black lowers the value of the hue.

Warm. Yellows, oranges, and reds comprise the warm half of the color wheel. These colors create the illusion of advancing when compared with their cooler counterparts. They also provide a warm, friendly sensation.

6

Using Color

"Color is a science, and its application an art."

The makeup artist and the portrait painter are, to a large degree, one and the same. Both must utilize the artistic elements of line, shading, composition, and color to create a work of art. Both must use pigments to express themselves, altering reality to encompass a desired, controlled end. In addition, both create a product that is weighed and evaluated by the public as to its "success."

One can hardly afford to take this comparison lightly. Certainly both must develop some ability in sketching to enable them to communicate visual ideas. Both need to comprehend shading and to use it in manipulating form. Beyond these basics, however, the alignment weakens. Color, the most important design element available to the artist, is rarely stressed in makeup. This chapter reestablishes this kinship, explaining how to select and use colors in creating complexion and dimension.

Though this approach employs an artistic use of color, one does not have to be a Rembrandt to use it with great control and success. One of the beautiful elements about color is its built-in "fudge factor." The eye will accept *lots* of color error before it registers a complaint. The exercises in this chapter move from very simple projects to more challenging. Travel at your own pace, digesting each step carefully before tackling the next.

Lest you think that you are about to enter a cosmetic twilight zone, it should be emphasized that both the pancake/grease approach and the color theory overlap to a large degree. Both employ the juxtaposition of lights and darks to create facial form. Both systems must balance contrast and intensity depending on the playing situation. Both deal with an enhancement or exaggeration of facial features, and both employ pigments to render expression on the human face. In fact, only the pureness of the colors and the order in which they are applied differ when comparing base approaches with the color system.

Color Application

With traditional approaches, the entire face, ears, neck, and other facial features are covered with a layer of flesh-tone cosmetic. This layer essentially flattens the face visually, obliterating any natural coloring and most of the texture in the complexion. Over this "base," one then applies highlight and shadow tones to recreate the lost dimension or create the illusion of new features. Lipsticks, eye shadow, and any other cosmetic needed to create age spots, wrinkles, and the like follow. Pushing pigment around on a pancake base can result in ragged blending on a dry complexion, while trying to work on a slippery grease surface can result in a smeared, muddy appearance. To help compensate for running, shining, and streaking, the makeup must often be powdered, which adds another layer that may further flatten out the final effect.

The color system relies on the eye's natural tendency to acknowledge and unite color, *supplementing* complexion rather than obliterating it. Hues are creamed *into* the skin, leaving only a *sensation* of color on the surface, not a layer of cosmetic. The color system utilizes colors on the face only where they are appropriate, rather than layering highlights and shadows on top of a base. This reduces cosmetic buildup, allows blending on the actual skin (which is easier to control than on a base), and provides for a more logical progression in creating form.

With the color system, the highlights are applied first, thus defining the subsequent structure of the features before the other makeup is added in support. Once the prominent areas have been applied accurately with the lightest color, they are "framed" with a second color. This "transitional" hue is, of course, darker than the first so as to make the highlights advance even more, but it is still lighter than the shadow color (which follows). This lowest value color is applied to the dips and hollows, which must appear to recede. With this controlled three-step process, the complexion range and structural definition are established simultaneously. Detail work can be rendered on this dimensional backdrop, followed, just as traditional methods should be, with a series of stipples.

There are several advantages to working with the color approach:

1. Premixed colors demand that actors or actresses often purchase dozens of complexion tones to accommodate the numerous roles they might play. This can become quite expensive. Since only three primaries are used (along with black and white) in the color system to achieve virtually *any* range of complexions, the makeup kit is drastically reduced in both volume and cost.

2. Again, because of the range of colors attained by mixing the primaries, the performer is not limited in imagination to only a manufactured offering of complexion tones.

3. Because the color approach advocates a very thin application of cream cosmetic, very little makeup is used. Streaking, running, and the need to powder and set the makeup are virtually eliminated.

4. The color approach works *with* the natural complexion rather than obliterating it, making it ideal for other than Caucasian performers. Black performers find this unique system reads with far more naturalness on their own skin than the cover-up approaches advocated by pancake and grease.

5. Color provides tremendous flexibility. One can circle the entire color wheel and slide up or down the value and intensity scales to accommodate intimate as well as long-play situations without forfeiting believability.

6. Color lends a vibrancy and richness that tease the human eye into accepting it as being more natural than the cover-up approaches.

All of the major manufacturers of theatrical makeup carry cosmetics in pure colors. Colored greasepaints and liquid are appropriate for stylized work or stipples, but for little else since they both read "heavy" on the face. The cream-based liners, which come in flat circular cases, or cream sticks, which are manufactured in push-up tubes, are ideal. Their consistency and color saturation are wonderful. They blend together well, come in a wide array of hues, do not need powdering, are gentle on the skin, and wipe or wash off easily.

Liners and sticks are available in dozens of luscious colors. Although it is fun and useful to include as many as you can afford in your makeup kit, only the following are necessary:

White is, of course, an essential color, since one frequently needs to lighten colors for use as highlights. Only a little white is generally needed to make a color "work" on the face. Too much leads to an area that flattens out or looks ghostly under stage lights.

Black may be needed occasionally to lower the value of a color, but as a rule it should be largely avoided. Since black is naturally not found at all on the human face, it tends to read as a "dead" spot. Dark greens, reds, or blues are far more effective in giving a lively sense of beard stipple, shadowing, or stylized work. Any design that requires linear detail work in black (such as a highly stylized project) would benefit more from a dry cake liner, which can be applied cleanly with a brush and will not smear.

The yellow, red, and blue found on the color wheel are too bright to be used directly on the face for realistic application. Though one could lower the intensity, precious time would be taken. For that reason, the primary range of colors includes hues that are already of a subdued intensity.

Yellows include Bob Kelly's "golden yellow," which is already a mustard color, Nye's "mellow yellow," or Mehron's "yellow #16."

Because most available *blues* are fairly light, they are not very effective as a shadow color, even when mixed with black. (They tend to gray out because of the white content.) Kelly makes a royal blue, which is both dark and intense in color. Though it can be brought up in value, it needs no black to perform as an effective shadow and wrinkle color direct from the container. Because it is so saturated, it combines easily with reds and yellows to produce lively colors.

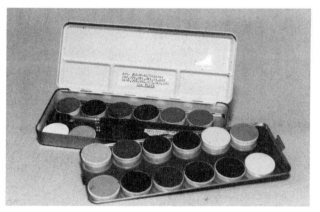

Figure 6–1.
Cream liners are manufactured by all the theatrical cosmetic companies in circular plastic containers. The Mehron company produces a five-color liner set (Figure 6–1b) that includes the pure primary colors, black, and white for a reasonable cost, while the Kryolan company produces sets with 12, 24, or 36 colors in them. These exciting colors can also be applied with a brush like water colors and dry in a flat matte finish.

Red is the most difficult color to select and work with. Bright reds tend to overpower other colors and glow on the face. In addition, reds seem to react differently with various people's complexions, making it a good idea to experiment. Nye's "dark tech" is probably the most effective red available, though Mehron's "dark lip rouge" is adequate. Stein's #13, "dark crimson," is a rich blood-red color that mixes well but that tends to stain some complexions. Useful colors in the red range—welcome additions to any kit—include Nye's "sunburn stipple," and Kelly's SR7, "healthy cheek blush."

Making the transition from more traditional approaches to pure color is sometimes made easier by integrating the two. The basic color approach can always be done over a pancake base, though freshness is forfeited. It can also be approached by actually mixing colors *with* grease or flesh-colored cream sticks. The first project describes this process.

Select a "flesh" color that nearly approximates your own flesh color and place it, along with red, yellow, white, and blue liners, on a counter in front of you. The initial project will entail only the reinforcement of your own features. Consequently, your self-portraits done in both line and shading will be helpful, and they should be taped to the mirror where you can refer quickly to them.

As you know from having done the light-dark projects on your face, the prominent areas will be lightest, while the natural recessions will be rendered in the darkest color. With the color approach, an intermediate color will be added to bridge the two, adding richness and making the transition smoother. To facilitate this project, review the various areas of the face, perhaps even penciling in each of the areas as has been done in Figure 6–3b. A bit of forethought and preplanning can save time and frustration later.

You may also refer to the "maps" in Figures 6–2a, b, and c. Each indicates general placement on the average face.

Ready to begin? Take the cream stick and wipe it across your palm, as indicated in Figure 6–3c. Because this color is so very near to your own complexion in value, it is necessary to lighten it so that it will work as a highlight color, and thus seem to "stand out" more than the other colors on the face. Do this by pulling your finger across the white liner and adding it to the color already in the palm.

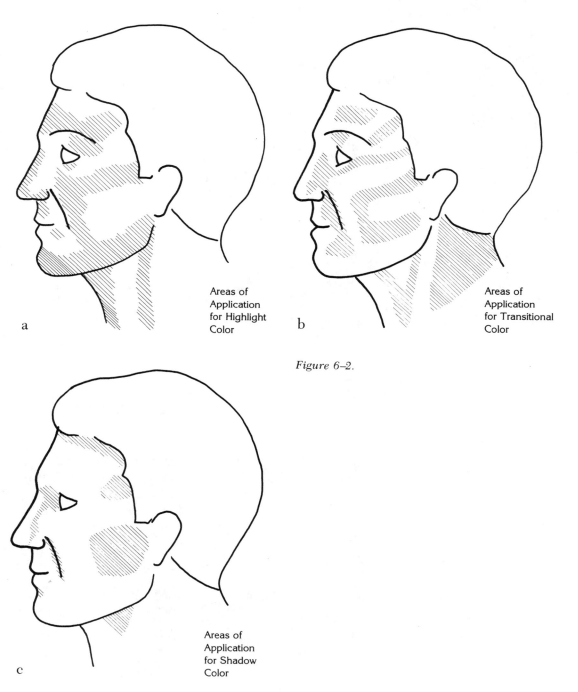

Areas of
Application
for Highlight
Color

a

Areas of
Application
for Transitional
Color

b

Figure 6–2.

Areas of
Application
for Shadow
Color

c

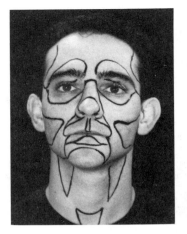

a

b

c

d

82

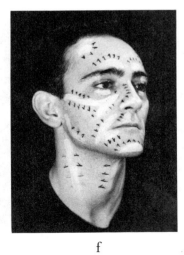

e

f

g

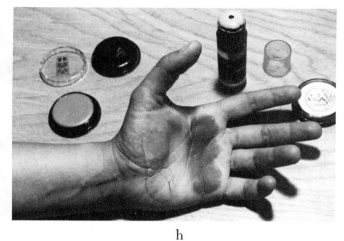

h

i

Figure 6–3.
The application of colors is often made easier if each area is designated on the face. Though Figure 6–3a indicates the areas very well, the application with an eyebrow pencil would be much too dark. The lines would show through the transparent makeup, smudging it and changing the colors.

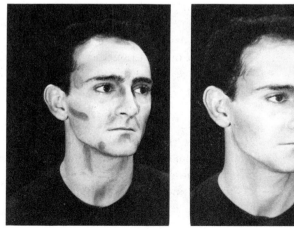

j

k

Now add a swipe of golden yellow to add color. (Yellow is also a warm color, which naturally advances toward the eye.) Figure 6–3d shows a palm with the original cream stick and the color that results from blending the three. Too much white will make the mixture look unnatural on the face, and too little will result in makeup that does not read appreciably lighter than the natural complexion. One must therefore learn how to gauge the proper proportions.

Wipe the finger nearly clean (refer to Figure 3–14, Chapter 3) and apply a strip of this highlight color to each area on the face that naturally advances. Refer to Figure 6–3e as a guide. Note that one strip is placed in the center of each area, rather than filling it. With a clean finger, pull the pigment outward as the arrows in Figure 6–3f illustrate. There should be just enough pigment to disappear into the adjacent flesh without leaving an edge. If there is too much cosmetic, you will end up with muddy or abrupt edges between colors. There should actually be so little makeup that none will come off on the back of a hand that is rolled gently across the face after blending.

For the next step, start with a clean palm and add another smear of the cream stick. This time, add the smallest bit of red to warm it up a bit. No white is necessary since this color does not need to advance more than the natural warmness provided by the red will allow. After wiping the finger again, merely "tap" this color onto the face where indicated in Figure 6–2b, adjacent to the lightest areas, but spilling slightly into those areas designated for the receding features. Figure 6–3g shows the face after this smooth application. The color, so close to the natural flesh, is barely detectible . . . as it should be.

Depending upon the amount of makeup left in the hand, royal blue may simply be added to the reddish hue to create a purple-like color. If little remains, blue may simply be added to more cream stick. The resulting color should be only slightly darker than the original cream stick. One may hold the hand near the face in the mirror (Figure 6–3i) to see whether this last color will be too dark or balance well with the first two applications. Place this darker color into the areas indicated in Figures 6–2c and 6–3j. Gently blend this shadow color from the center outwards toward the transitional color. The resulting application should read with the uninterrupted smoothness shown in Figure 6–3k.

If the application looks good, hurray for you! If not, let's consider some of the potential problems.

1. You may simply be using too much pigment. Remember to keep the colors very thin on the face so that natural texture and color show through. As with a transparent watercolor, trying to rework or wipe off existing color usually results in a muddy, overworked appearance.

2. If the overall sensation is one of blotchiness, perhaps you are using too little pigment, and you don't have an adequate amount to blend outward. If you don't use enough pigment, you may end up with ragged spots of color or with areas of exposed flesh. Another cause might be dry skin, which absorbs the pigment before it can be creamed into the skin. A "base" of lotion or skin cream will help.

3. The most common problem that plagues makeup application is simply uneven blending. If you can blend the colors together with no indication of where one begins and the other ends, you have already solved 90 percent of the problems associated with any application. Areas should flow together as easily as they do on the natural face, even when using exaggerated contrasts. If it will help to return to paper and charcoal for practice, by all means do so.

4. One reason makeup may not read well is that the natural anatomy has been violated. Try to make use of one's own facial structure whenever possible. Placing a highlight color in the center of a fold, or a dark color on the bridge of the nose to create a totally new form, does not always read well. Remember that there are limitations to how much one can convincingly alter natural contours in a fully lit situation where natural shadows come into play.

5. If the highlight, transitional, and shadow colors are not all equal distances apart on a value scale, the makeup may read in an awkward manner. Refer to the examples in Plate 16, which shows the lightest and darkest colors balanced well on either side of the center color. Colors which lie close to one another—that is, have little contrast—are necessary for general enhancement. Greater contrast, such as that found with old age or reconstruction, demand lighter lights and darker darks to read well. If one color is much lighter or much darker than both of the others, it will stand out awkwardly, calling attention to itself.

6. The intensity of all colors must also be relatively equal in makeup. As Plate 15 shows, one color that is "louder" than all the rest can destroy the makeup. In most cases, colors applied to the face are of a medium to low intensity. Bright colors are utilized mostly for stylized applications, such as for clowns.

With practice, you will quickly learn to what degree you can move up or down the value and intensity scales. Your blending skills will quickly improve, and your confidence with color usage along with them. As you learn to gauge audience readibility, your knowledge and experience will begin to show in your makeup.

Next attempt the same project without the cream stick. Utilize only the three primary colors and white to subtly reinforce the natural features. Add a bit of white to the yellow for the highlights. Rather than use the red straight from the container, simply add a bit to the first yellow-white mixture, creating a peach color, which will work well for the transition. Again, rather than start with pure blue, add it to the peach mixture, tempering it a bit. In this way, the colors will be softer and relate to one another better. Remember to keep the blending smooth, and the application light and transparent. The final effect should not be unlike the initial attempt, except that the skin will have a fresher, less mask-like effect.

Selecting Color Schemes

This three-step approach—using a light color (or warm hue), a medium value color, and a darker color (or cool hue)—is basic to all color application. The illusions created with lights and darks in Chapter 3 remain the same, although colors are substituted for

1

2

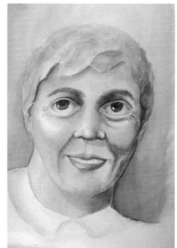

Plate 5
Can you tell which half of this actress's face is made up in color, and which half is a pancake application?

5

6

7

Plate 8
Home House Society Trustees,
courtesy Courtauld Institute
Galleries, London (Courtauld
Collection).

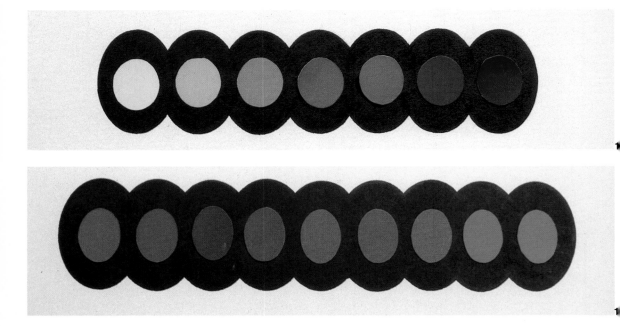

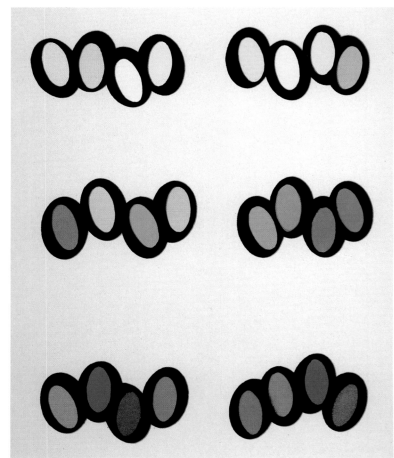

Plate 12 (top)
Value scale—adding white to red moves it up on the value scale, producing pink, while the addition of black lowers the value, resulting in a maroon color.

Plate 13 (center)
Intensity scale—by adding green to its complement, red, both are measurably dulled until a grey hue is obvious.

Plate 14 (right)
(Top row) A tint of any color, cool or warm, will advance toward the viewer. (Middle row) In a pure bright range directly off the color wheel, warm colors advance, while cool colors recede. (Bottom row) When used in conjunction with warm colors, low values of yellows, oranges, and reds seem to recede. Low values of a cool color recede with any color scheme.

Plate 15 (top)

The teeter-totter on the left employs three very intense colors for a makeup for the "little green sprout" in a childrens' play. Though the colors are bright, they work well together because they are balanced in brightness. The teeter-totter on the right balances as well, because all of the colors, though duller in intensity, are approximately the same brightness (or dullness in this case). The center figure would not read well on the stage. Because the yellow is so much brighter than the other two colors, it would pull focus away from them.

Plate 16 (bottom)

This chart indicates balance where color value is concerned. In order for all the colors to work well together on the face, the range must vary the same distance from the center color when lowering value as well as raising it. Top left figure shows a well-balanced three-color scheme for a youthful complexion. Top right figure indicates a range for old age, where higher highlights and lower values as well are necessary to achieve a maximum of dimension. Bottom left figure is unbalanced at the highlight end of the scale. This pink would tend to glow in comparison to the other two relatively low value hues. The opposite is true of bottom right figure where the low value color is too dark to work well with the other colors. Lowering the transitional color just a bit on the value scale would quickly remedy this and balance the colors out a bit more.

15

16

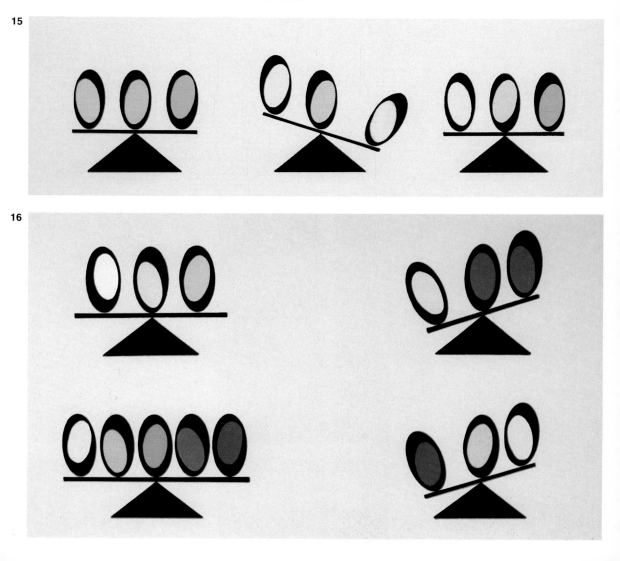

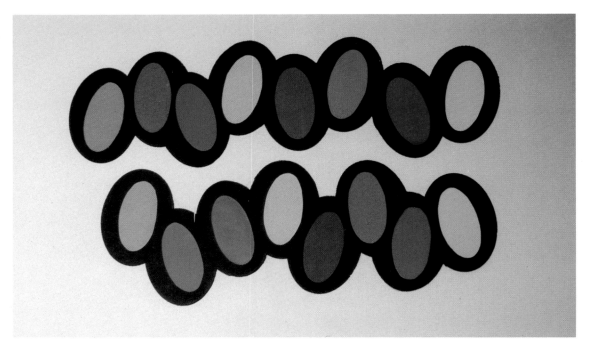

Plate 17 (above)
The very intense colors in the top row would be too loud for most natural complexions. One
is usually wiser to select colors of a lower intensity. Hues such as those in the bottom row
work quite well for normal playing situations.

18   **19**

20

21

22

23

24

25

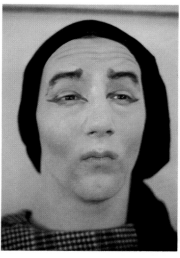

charcoal and chalk. Contrast and complexion ranges are created solely by the variety of colors selected for use. Plates 18 through 25 in the color section illustrate several basic color schemes and actual makeups done with each selection. Three colors are indicated for the basic foundation beneath each makeup. The fourth color swatch is the color used for the final stipple, a procedure that does wonderful things in concluding any makeup and that will be covered later in this chapter. Using these as examples, try each, following the same steps used for the first project in this chapter.

Triad Scheme. The first scheme (Plates 18 and 19) is known as a *triad* scheme, and it is identical in color selection to the project you have just completed. A triad scheme utilizes any three colors that equally distant from one another on the color wheel. In each case, the warmest color (in this case yellow) is used for the highlights, while the coolest color is utilized for shading. The remaining color (in this case red) is used as the transition color.

Monochromatic Scheme. The second color scheme is known as a *monochromatic* scheme, as shown in Plates 20 and 21. This approach utilizes only one color in three different values. One may select any color from the color wheel, both raising and lowering it in value to create colors for the three steps or simply to play in either direction. Plate 21, for instance, demanded a very light and delicate complexion. The darkest color was therefore at about the middle of the value range. A little white was added for the transitional color, while a great deal was necessary for the highlight. A dark swarthy complexion might demand three color variations from the middle to the lowest end of the value scale. It is advisable to mix the intermediate color first when working with this color scheme. Some of the color can then be pulled to another portion of the palm and raised in value, while yet another sample can be lowered in value. One can thus be more assured of color consistency than by trying to match the colors as one goes along.

To add a little more life to his makeup, the actor in Plate 22 combined the triad approach with a monochromatic scheme. He mixed a light value and a low value from the original sienna color. He then selected a yellow and a blue to complement the reddish tone. As with the first makeup project, he added the yellow to the high-value sienna, while adding a bit of blue to the shadow color. The resulting sienna has a richer, more lively look because of the additional color.

Complementary Scheme. The character in Plate 23 has employed a *complementary* color scheme by using colors that lie across the color wheel from one another: yellows and purples, greens and reds, and, in this case, oranges and blues. Lively contrast can be achieved in this manner since adjacent complements tend to intensify one another.

Analogous Scheme. Another scheme to guarantee that all the colors will relate well is an *analagous* scheme. One simply needs to divide the color wheel into thirds and to utilize the colors lying next to one another within that segment. Plate 24 is done with colors from the yellow-green portion of the wheel, while Plate 25 uses colors in the red-blue range.

Try examples from each of these color schemes, seeing which read best on your own complexion. Don't be dismayed if things don't look perfect the first time. Working with color and seeing it in the mirror may seem a bit strange to begin with. Always step back, however, to view the final makeup from a distance to get a more accurate perspective. And remember that the fourth step in the application process can usually resurrect even the most wayward application . . . a stipple. Done with a nonporous sponge created especially for this purpose, the stipple should not be overlooked in *any* approach to makeup. It not only returns the texture to the face that fades under makeup and distance, but it serves as a panacea for many problems in doing makeup.

As with any technique, there are definitely right and wrong ways to apply a stipple. A proper coverage is indicated in Figure 6–4b. A stipple of one or more colors should be subtle, giving the face a sensation of texture and heightened coloration without being obvious. This is accomplished by mixing a small bit of color in the palm of the hand and wiping the flat of the stipple sponge across it, as in Figure 6–4c, so that color is picked up evenly on the tiny points of the sponge. It is then pressed against the face in random, overlapping patterns. Picking up color directly from a container of

a

b

c

Figure 6–4.

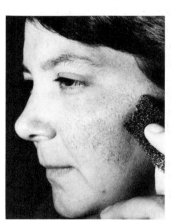

d

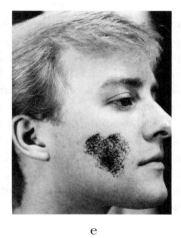

e

f

cosmetic will often result in blobs of color on the face (Figure 6–4e), which needless to say is not very desirable. Dragging or pulling the sponge while pressing results in directional, obvious lines—also not desirable. If the coverage is not even, blotches appear, which seem to fracture the face (Figure 6–4f). With a bit of practice (and sometimes rounding off the sharp corners of the sponge with scissors), you should soon be able to control the coverage and utilize stipples in one of many ways.

The human face becomes richer in coloration, texture, and surface irregularities as it ages. Our eyes are used to this phenomenon, and thus we notice something is amiss when the surface is smooth and even. To combat the effects of any makeup, as well as to create the illusion of age, stipples can be employed. Figure 6–5 shows a young man with a flawlessly smooth complexion who simply added a stipple to effectively age his skin. This is, of course, the most obvious use for stipples, though they can also be used to create dimension, to alter color, and to blend colors.

Bland makeup can be seemingly intensified with a stipple. Using a complementary color over a basic three-color scheme will make it seem livelier. A dull yellow complexion will have more life if a gentle purple stipple is applied, just as an area done in a dull blue will seem to be brighter if stippled with orange.

When used correctly, stipples can be used to "punch up" areas that are weak. If an area of highlight doesn't advance quite enough to read properly, stipple it with a very light color rather than layer it with more pigment. The effect will be much richer in that the original color will show through the tiny dots of the lighter color, lending more depth. Using a very dark color will by the same token "deepen" a hollow or crevice. Figure 6–6m in the old age sequence illustrates this well. Note in Figure 6–4b that the young actor has used stipples exclusively to create a sense of dimension over a pancake base.

Sometimes the colors on the face do not seem to balance. A highlight may be too light in comparison to the other two colors, or perhaps the transitional color is more intense than the other two, shouting for attention. Stippling can easily solve these problems (if they are not *too* colossal) by seemingly pulling the colors into alignment. One simply needs to stipple over the offending color

Figure 6–5.

with one or both of the other colors . . . or stipple the two weaker hues with the problem color, depending on the desired effect.

Stippling can also serve to blend the colors on the face when the edges are a bit ragged. Stippling over the entire face with the transitional color, or in fact, any color, will coax the eye into flowing more smoothly over the surface.

The eye can be tricked into transferring color without complete coverage. If the chosen complexion range isn't a drastic departure from the original skin coloring, one can extend the colors onto the neck, ears, chest, and arms in the form of a stipple, and the eye will be convinced that every inch of exposed flesh is, in fact, covered with makeup. This color conveyance only works, of course, when the high-value, warm colors are used in the receding areas. A tint used in the cleavage will do little to convey a buxom beauty of the 1800s.

In a quick-change situation when the quality of the makeup needs to change, alterations can often be made with stipples placed right over the original application. The result is often more convincing than trying to layer on an additional coating of cosmetic or removing the original. A red stipple is very convincing when one needs to create a burned effect. A stipple of blue-gray will turn a healthy complexion into a sick one in seconds, while a peach or rose color will immediately "warm" up a cool complexion. A ghoulish transformation can be suggested with a green stipple, especially when emphasized by a lighting gel of a pale green hue. Ye-e-e-ch!

Color stippling can also be used in a way that is adopted from the pointalist painters. If you look closely at the painting in Plate 8, you will see that it is done with tiny dots of color. The entire canvas seems to flow softly together as the eye is teased from area to area. As we learned in Chapter 4 on color, we see many varied hues within each color. A painting that includes an apple painted in red, a vase painted in blue, and a lemon rendered with yellow will look abrupt and unpleasant to the eye until washes or bits of each color are introduced over the others. This is exactly what the painter has done in Plate 8 to give it a sense of realism. The blue of the dress is also found in the table, mirror, and walls, while the brown coloring used predominantly in the table can be found in the walls, hair, and elsewhere. Stippling the entire makeup with any single color immediately tends to tie the entire face together. Yet when colors are used that are found in the costume or scenery, the visual illusion is extended in a pleasing manner to even greater limits.

The idea with any stipple is, of course, to be subtle, so that the eye registers a soft coordination of color sensations. Be sensitive in your applications and you can provoke many illusions as well as solve application problems in a lively, exciting manner. Experiment with a variety of colored stipples over your bases done in each color scheme and catalog the results. You may be quite surprised at the effects one can get with colors. The combinations are certainly endless.

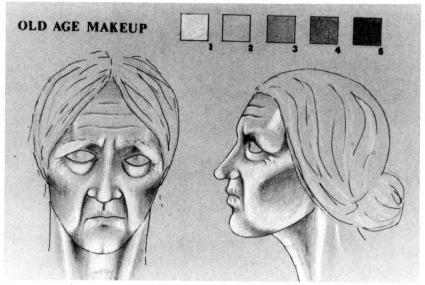

Figure 6–6a.

When doing old age makeup, great contrast is necessary. For that reason, this facial map includes a very light stipple as well as a very dark color for wrinkles and effective stippling. This map was created with the performer's own features in mind and rendered in colored pencils. The hues include light lavendar, a rose color, and a dark lavendar. This project is completed in color in Plates 26 through 31.

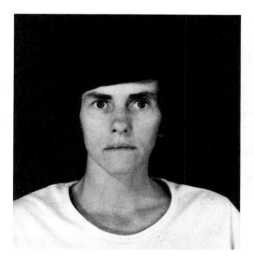

Figure 6–6b.
This is, of course, the actress with no makeup. In a matter of a few steps, she will age forty years.

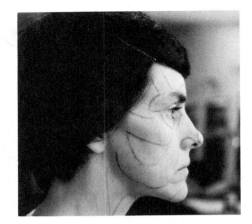

Figure 6–6c.
The first step in complex makeup is sketching various areas on the actual face, creating lines and shapes that can be followed with the makeup.

Figure 6–6d.
The lightest color is blended in the palm and placed on those areas that advance the most (see Plate 26): the bridge of the nose, the bags beneath the eyes, the cheek bones, the chin, the nasalabials, and the eyelids. Note also that the prominent features of the neck have been included.

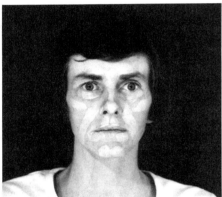

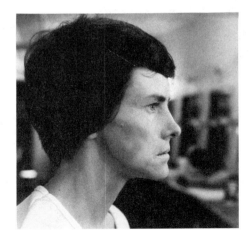

Figure 6–6e.
Once blended, the medium-rose color is tapped into the highlights, smoothly pulling them together, while extending into the face hollows as well.

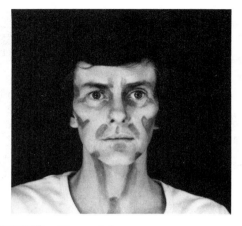

Figure 6–6f.
A dark purple-rose color is then
placed on those areas that must
seem to recede: the nasalabial
crease, the cheek hollows, the
temples, the sides of the nose,
under the bottom lip, beneath the
bags, and under the eyebrows
near the nose. The jaw line is
determined, and the "V" areas in
the neck are accentuated.

Figure 6–6g

Figure 6–6g,h (right), i (p. 96).
Once the darks are blended into
the transitional color, areas with
particular depth must be given
attention. Working with a brush,
folds and creases are emphasized,
while the deepest portions of the
structure are again reinforced for
more punch.

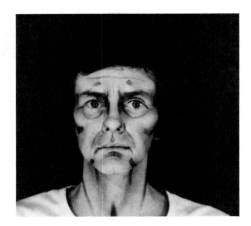

Figure 6–6i.

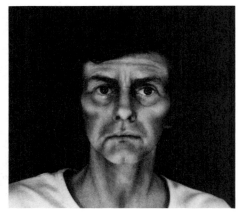

Figure 6–6j.
Working with both the finger and a brush, these areas are smoothly blended.

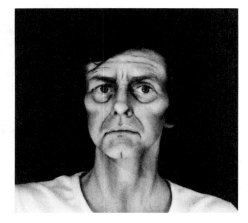

Figure 6–6k.
Sometimes deep areas need several applications. Here, nasalabials, eye bags, the chin cleft, and forehead wrinkles are again stated and blended.

Figure 6–6l.

Figure 6–6l (above), m (left). Once the structure and wrinkle work is complete, a stipple or two (or sometimes three) is needed. Note the difference when a very light color is used to emphasize the skeletal structure and baggy protuberances, while a deep purple-blue adds punch to the hollows and folds.

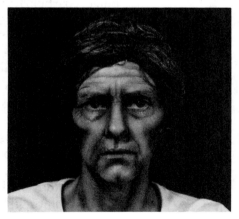

Figure 6–6n. A wig and hairnet complete the illusion.

One can't very effectively pick any old scheme for a character and expect it to read appropriately on the stage. Everyone possesses a unique complexion range, which reflects our age, health, race, nationality, heredity, and the climate in which we reside. Looking through a magazine or observing people around you will quickly affirm this. Some have a ruddy quality to their complexion, while others are more olive in coloration. A yellowish sensation dominates some people's skin coloring, while others tend to be more in the lavendar range. Coloring in the complexions of blacks ranges from a yellowish or reddish hue to a color sensation of purple or blue. With so many colors to choose from, it may seem confusing to select only three and to be assured that together they will work when combined with your own skin tones to provide exactly the right complexion tone on stage.

Understanding how colors read is a vital step in color selection. We already know that warm colors (the reds, oranges, and yellows) read in a friendly, inviting manner, while the cool hues of green, purple, and blue do not. Beyond that, let's break the colors down in more detail:

Yellow is a good general-purpose color for highlights on healthy flesh. It adds a brightness and a warmth when used as a stipple. It is the logical base choice for many stereotypic Oriental complexions. When used in a grayed-out intensity, it provides a wonderful color for extremely unhealthy or jaundiced skin.

Orange is a lively, energetic color. Any color in the orange range, particularly a peach-tone, is a good choice for a healthy complexion.

Red is an intense color that suggests rage, violence, or passion. When used in excess (and it doesn't take much to be excessive), it creates a sore, burned impression. In moderation, however, it quickly warms up the complexion. Red-browns are excellent for ruddy complexions. Used in the pink or pink-lavendar range, reds provide a delicate glow.

Blue, when used in the blue-gray range, is an excellent choice for a ghastly, ill look. When used in the low-value range, such as royal blue straight from the container, blue serves as an excellent shadow and wrinkle color, since the eye accepts blue very well. It provides an exciting beard stubble color when used in conjunction with other low-value colors such as maroon, and it is a very effective stipple color for creating hollows. Because the royal blue is so dark in value, it can be added to other colors not only to lower them in value, but to alter the color just a bit for dynamic shadow work.

Purples are excellent choices for creating a frail, thin-skinned look, such as one might find in very old age or in a youth protected from the sun. Purple, with its touch of red, makes an excellent shadow color on the average complexion.

Greens are not a terribly useful color on their own for doing makeup, as they often instill a sickly, unnatural look. However, when pushed into the blue-green range or combined with yellow, green provides a good color for olive complexions or shading on Oriental skin tones. Dark greens are useful for a beard stubble and stippling of old or sickly complexions.

Beyond these general applications and suggestions, there are no pat formulas for color selection. You should select a color scheme based on the answers to the following questions:

1. *What is the character's health?* If the role suggests a poor state of health, cool colors might be the best choice. Appropriate warmth could be achieved with warm stipples. Colors in the warm range are preferred for a character who is healthy and robust.

2. *What sort of climate does this character reside in?* If the character is of a type that spends much time outdoors in the sun, the warmth will reflect in his or her complexion. Someone who stays indoors or who lives where there is little sunshine could be rather pale.

3. *What is the nationality of the character being played? Is he or she of a particular race?* We tend to think of the people from the Mediterranean area as having an olive range in complexion, while the Oriental skin tends to be a bit more sallow. Some American Indians have a yellow-orange or reddish-brown hue to their complexions. Rather than applying these stereotypic colors automatically, however, refer to pictures of people from various nations and of different racial stocks. You will be amazed at the variation.

4. *Is the personality manifested by this character of a warm, inviting nature, or cool and aloof?* Someone of a gentle, fragile nature might be expressed with delicate, smooth colors, while the complexion of a rugged, grisly person might be rendered in darker colors, employing many stipples.

5. *What age is the actor?* The flesh of youth demands a somewhat lighter and more delicate palette than aged skin. Blue veins are more visible with age. Blood vessels break, leaving small red stains, while dark spots appear, leaving the skin looking mottled in older people.

Answering these questions should at least suggest a color range. More information can be gleaned from the makeup analysis explained in the following chapters. It might help in color selection to visit your local friendly paint store and gather dozens or even hundreds of color swatches. Arrange them according to their placement on the color wheel and refer to them when making selections. Actually seeing the colors is often a great aid in formulating schemes that will work effectively with your own skin tones.

As a review and as an aid in the selection process, keep in mind all we *do* know about color.

1. A minimum of three colors is necessary to effectively "sculpt" dimension on the human face.

    a. One of these colors must seem to advance more than the other two. This color must therefore be lighter and/or warmer than the transitional and shadow hue.

    b. One of the colors must seem to recede as viewed by the human eye in order to work effectively as a shadow color. It must therefore be darker and/or cooler than the other two colors.

    c. The third color, known as the transitional or intermediate color, must fall midway between the other two on the value scale.

2. Additional colors are useful. Colors of extreme lightness or darkness may be necessary for the ultimate in contrasts, as is sometimes necessary with old age.

3. Stipples allow considerable leeway in color selection. They can provide additional color, warmth, texture, coolness, or intensity when used over the basic color foundation.

4. All of the colors used on the face must be balanced. Each must be of equal intensity, with none of the colors blatantly brighter than the others.

5. The highlight color and the color used for shadow work must be equally distant on the value scale from the transitional color. Refer to Plates 15 and 16 as a refresher on balancing value and intensity

6. Although there are thousands of colors, sticking to a particular scheme for the basic foundation will help tie all the colors together in a functional way.

7

Reading the Human Face

A controlled application of cosmetics is, of course, only part of the artistic process. Even the most exquisite application is little more than street makeup if it fails to fully develop the character being played.

A believably haggard old face of sixty, staring sullenly back from the mirror of a young actress, can do much to help her become thoroughly absorbed in a role. It can serve as the key to unlock the audience's most deepfelt emotions—inciting their adoration, provoking their loathing, and insuring the pitiful actress of their sympathy.

One must not underestimate the power of the facial image on the viewer. People are prone to a curiosity and interest as they observe the faces around them, judging for themselves what kinds of persons reside within. The performer must, with makeup, provide as many clues as possible.

"A man may be known by his look, and one that hath understanding of his countenance when one meetest him." Ancient literature indicates that "reading" a person by his face was a common practice. It most probably began long before recorded history, and it will undoubtedly persist as long as humankind exists. The term to describe this fascination is *physiognomy*. Many branches have

103

sprouted from this main trunk over the centuries to explore the relationship between animal and human faces, to experiment with the laws of muscular motion, and even to analyze the bumps on one's head! It would seem that humans have been insatiable in their need to find a pattern in the structure of a person's face that would instantly reveal the character of the mind.

"Face reading" first became an honored profession in the classical age, when philosophers such as Plato wrote in depth on the subject. So convincing were their studies relating personality traits to particular features that even Pythagoras wouldn't allow students into his academy unless their faces indicated that they might profit from his instruction!

After being confused with astrology, magic, and sorcery during the Dark Ages, scientists of the thirteenth century strove to give it "scientific respectability." Seeking to denounce the hocus pocus associated with face reading, astrologer Michael Scot published the first book on the subject. Winning the dubious title of "the father of modern physiognomy," Scott advocated the intriguing method of telling character by stretching the forehead wrinkles and letting them drop. So much for hocus pocus.

Figure 7–1.
Books on physiognomy in the 18th and 19th centuries often used illustrations such as this to correlate human faces and their relationship to the animal kingdom.

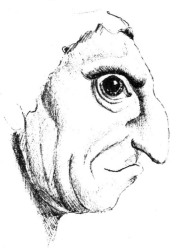

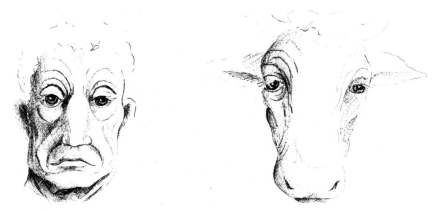

Figure 7–2.
Do you know anyone who resembles an animal, bird, or reptile?

The intrigue had become an obsession by the Renaissance. Artists such as Da Vinci believed that proportions and mathematical formulas applied to the face would reveal character, and he painted and sculpted according to these theories. Authors such as Dryden and Milton employed such physiognomical detail that we can't help but believe that persons were truly judged by their features. As Shakespeare's Duncan noted, "There is no art to find a man's construction in the face."

By the late 1700s, books abounded on the subject. None was so influential as that by Lavater, a poet, preacher, and painter. Because of his "scientific" studies, no woman would marry without first consulting Lavater's book. No shopkeeper would take on a clerk, or any household a servant. The preoccupation with facial

Figure 7–3.
For centuries, artists analyzed form variation in the human face, formulating proportions that were "indicative" of certain types and personalities. From Da Vinci to Durer, these coordinates were consciously applied to canvas to aid the viewer in understanding the characterizations.

 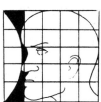 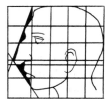 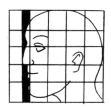

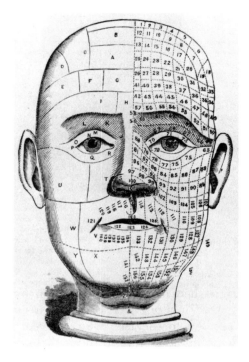

Figure 7–4.
A popular chart found in the works on physiognomy included this proportional human face. Each area was designated a particular characteristic that was, or was not attributed to the person depending upon the development of that small area. A person with a soft cushion over his or her left ear, for instance, could be counted on to keep a secret!

structure so dominated society, that many would not appear on a public street without dropping cloth bags over their heads!

By 1830, criminologists devised charts that specified physical traits indicative of illegal or immoral behavior in order to categorize criminals. Physiognomical tests were administered into this century on Ellis Island to classify the immigrating population according to their intelligence. As a result, thousands of persons were institutionalized for no faults greater than the shape of their lips or foreheads.

Books abounded on face reading at the turn of the twentieth century, and their influence on characterization in the theatre may have been profound, if one uses theatrical makeup texts as evidence. Such books, written into the 1930s, reveal such "truths" as "long noses are possessed by unemotional characters," or "the drooping of the inner half of the eyebrow is common in virtuous nuns." What can one expect from a generation that believed tobacco contributed to protruding ears, and "*all* Chinese have prominent teeth due to the excessive drinking of tea"!

One particularly amusing book was written by Samuel Wells in 1984. His deliberations on actors are perhaps noteworthy. "They exhibit a delight in catering to the low and sensual, glorifying the animal rather than the spiritual. . . . Few out of 100 would pass for decent citizens, much less for circumspect Christians! . . . They are no more than miserable abortions of humanity." Actors had better hope that the popularity of physiognomy does not soon return!

Figure 7–5a.
This collection of "sordid" actors appeared in Hewlett's book on physical "types."

Figure 7–5b.
"Cursed be the actor." This drawing clearly demonstrates that the actor is far inferior to the doctor, largely due to the pitifully under-developed state of the actor's forehead.

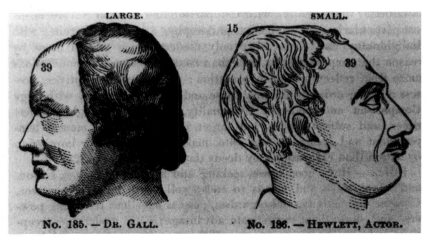

No. 185. — Dr. Gall.   No. 186. — Hewlett, Actor.

Though we find such generalizations a bit far-fetched and somehow antiquated, doesn't each one of us make certain assumptions almost daily based on the faces of people we encounter? We cannot help but find bits of the human features that, because of our own life experiences, trigger emotional or mental responses. We find ourselves feeling scared, trusting, or even disgusted as we encounter various people. We are constantly compiling character notes from the manner and features of those around us, including those we observe on the stage.

Devising that "proper" face for each character in a play is largely the job of the makeup artist, and it is not always an easy task. The human response to the face is based on our own experience, conditioning, and cultural information. The media have a tremendous impact on our assessment of what is attractive and what is not. It also reinforces our ideas of stereotypes. Each of us has images in mind of what "the thug," "the cover girl," the "shameless hussy," and the "grizzled cowpoke" look like because of the way these types have been portrayed in books, in movies, and on television. To some degree, casting people that fit these types, or designing makeup that lends that credibility, assures that the audience will relate to them in a predictable manner. There is a drawback, however, in promoting the stereotype, as it tends to limit the playing range of the performer. One expects certain behavior from a "mobster" or from the weak, virginal heroine, and the average audience member may have difficulty with this very established type doing or saying things that don't fit the viewer's mental image.

The musical *Guys and Dolls* is populated with stereotypes: the innocent heroine, the aging showgirl, the dashing, rich hero. and an assortment of street-wise gamblers. The show is light and fun, playing on the expected. With a show like this, where the audience expects stereotypes, the production might be weakened by trying to give the characters more visual substance.

In most cases, however, stereotypic makeup and behavior only stifle the role being played. Nationalities and races have suffered from this method of easy categorization. Many of us have been conditioned to carry around mental images of what an Irishman should look like—or a Scandanavian, an Italian, or an Oriental. Along with a visual image comes an expectation of how they should talk and act. Some of these images may be accurate of *some* individuals within these categories, but by no means the majority. Utilize only those features that are necessary to convey the script as a total piece. In the *Moon for the Misbegotten*, where script references inform us that the characters are Irish, it could be confusing to make them up to look like Italians. In this case, promoting a bit of the stereotype will help the audience relate to the loud father and his wiry daughter.

Don't rely on the audience to fill in all the blanks, however. Every person is an individual, and one must select and combine features that will convey as much about that particular person as possible. Certainly we must take the media image into account, consider the effect of stereotypes on our thinking, and utilize our own personal experience. Yet these must all be balanced in a way that will convey as much information as possible to a broad range of individual audience members.

A wonderful exercise that broadens one's facial vocabulary entails sitting on a busy street or in a mall and closely observing the people who pass by. Doing this with a few friends is even more valuable as you will quickly find your own personal biases and reservations as you share notes. Try to ignore the clothes your "subjects" are wearing, as "costumes" are strong visual clues in themselves. Imagine what each person does for a living, what kind of a house (or tent, trailer, or teepee) they live in, whether they have children, what kind of hobbies they might enjoy, and whether they would be easy or difficult to talk with. As you make mental and written notes, ask yourself "why"? What about that person's face would make you want to talk to them, shy away from them, share a thought, or go to dinner? Does someone appear more intelligent because of the cut of his hair or the fact that she is wearing glasses? What gives you the impression that a person is an athlete, a professor, or a hooker?

a   b   c

d   e   f

Figure 7–6.
The human face is marvelously unique and intriguing, each one revealing clues as to that person's life experiences, personality, job, and so forth. What kind of a person does each face reveal? What would you imagine each does for a living? Which would you want to spend time chatting with and why?

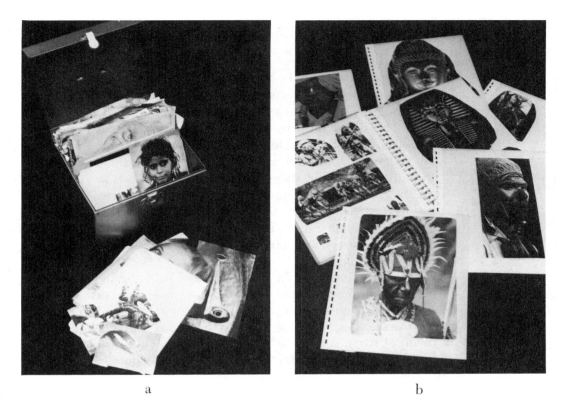

a   b

Figure 7–7.
The morgue one compiles may be organized in one of several different formats. One may keep the pictures in large envelopes, put them in scrapbooks, or file them in a large box. In any event, labels should be large and clear and the individual pictures should be loose so that any one can be quickly removed, placed in a plastic folder to protect it from makeup, and used in designing or applying makeup.

Note that a different combination of similar features can create quite a different impression. Angular eyebrows of bushy proportions on one may look mean when combined with small beady eyes and a tight mouth. On another, combined with a swollen red nose and smiling mouth, they might lend a docile, inane look.

A wealth of information can be gathered by spending a few hours analyzing the faces that pass by. Compile a notebook complete with sketches to refer to when reading plays and visually defining roles. No makeup artist can hope to be able to design appropriate and detailed makeup without the visuals so necessary for reference.

It helps tremendously to maintain a file in which you keep all of your sketches, drawings, and notes done in class or "on assign-

111

ment." In addition, tear sheets from magazines, papers, photocopies from books, and photographs should be saved. Such a collection, referred to as a *morgue*, is a valuable addition to every performer's file. Many theatres maintain a morgue for research as well. The collection may be divided into units for easy reference: "animals," "youth," "middle age," "old age," "stylized," "complexion ranges," "special effects," "monsters and fiction," "scars and wounds," and "hair styles." In addition, sections might feature pictures showing how makeup was worn for various periods of history, articles written on skin or hair care, photographs from actual productions, or cosmetic information obtained from theatrical manufacturers. A thorough collection will prove its value time and time again.

One enterprising director who was having difficulty pulling the proper characterization she wanted from her cast of *Spoon River Anthology* arrived at a rehearsal with her car trunk filled with magazines. Each of the cast members was playing several different parts, and she felt that their concept of each was unclear, leading to a lack of communication and understanding among all the members of various scenes. She unloaded the stacks with the assignment. "Find a picture, or a composite of pictures (the eyes from one, the nose from another, and so on) that looks like each of the characters you are playing." The project sounded like fun, and the cast dove into the magazines with enthusiasm. The next hour was the most productive and revealing of any of the rehearsals. As they found a picture that they felt expressed a certain characteristic, they would share it, sometimes finding that the other cast members hadn't envisioned him or her that way at all! Many ideas and valuable thoughts were shared, including the personality found in various facial characteristics. By the end of the evening, each cast member had a clear idea of what the character looked like, as well as that of each of the other roles. The difference in both the acting and the cohesiveness of the production was immediately apparent. Stronger characterization emerged from the session, and tenuous relationships became strong and clear. In addition, each actor and actress had visuals to work from when it came time to formulate effective makeup for the role. Pictures certainly *can* be worth a thousand words, particularly when one starts to compile a facial map, as we shall see in the following chapter.

8

Facial Maps

The actor squinted at his reflection in the mirror, leaning back in his chair to obtain a perspective that would somehow flatter his makeup. Shaking his head, he tipped forward and vigorously rubbed away the shakey lines he had repeatedly applied. Now, with the base thoroughly smeared from his attempts, he rose to wash his face and begin again.

At the other end of the makeup counter, a confident actress tipped her face to check every angle on the makeup she had just completed. She smiled with pleasure, rose, and departed for the wardrobe. Securely taped to her mirror, amid several magazine clippings of noses and eyes, hung a makeup map.

Figure 8–1.

Newcomers to a large city would hardly think of trying to find their way around without the benefit of a street map. Yet many performers, like the young actor, attempt to apply makeup without adequately preparing a makeup map for guidance. The result of such negligence is not only confusion and frustration, but the loss of valuable time as well. A carefully prepared makeup map will assure that regardless of who applies the makeup from performance to performance, the outcome will remain consistent, be done efficiently, and provide the greatest sense of characterization possible.

Figures 8–2a, b, and c are pages one and two of a facial map. As you can see, they are essentially detailed worksheets where all the analytical and artistic problems can be worked out *before* dress rehearsal. At that point, it is simply a matter of sitting down and transferring the visual information from the map onto the performer's face.

Facial maps are vital in coordinating the makeup for a production to insure that the performers look as though they are all in the same production! Too often cast members apply their makeup differently. One will look garish, another barely "reads," while another appears quite stylized in comparison. Needless to say, this is not desirable. Facial maps are also a wonderful psychological push. Regardless of how small a part is, going through the process of creating a character on a facial map lends a great sense of a more fully developed and important character. Suddenly "munchkin number 8" takes on a more individualized and interesting part.

Then layout of the facial maps in this book provides an organized format that insures that every potential problem will be given consideration before any cosmetic is actually applied. You may want to duplicate them, or perhaps use them as a guide in devising maps that suit your own particular needs.

Page one includes the technical aspects of the production that may influence makeup. "Production," "Date" (of the performance), "Performer," and "Character" head the page. These are all useful pieces of information when one is keeping a file for research or as a permanent record as is kept by some actors or theatres. Attaching a photo of the finished makeup to the map provides useful information or impetus for later makeup assignments.

PRODUCTION   DATE

CHARACTER   PERFORMER

PERIOD

SHOW STYLE

THEATRE

LIGHTING

AGE

TEMPERAMENT

NATIONALITY/RACE

HEALTH

PROFESSION

ENVIRONMENT

CLIMATE

DISTINGUISHING FEATURES

EYES/EYEBROWS

MOUTH

CHEEKS

NOSE

CHIN/JAW

FOREHEAD

HAIR

OTHER

Figure 8–2a.

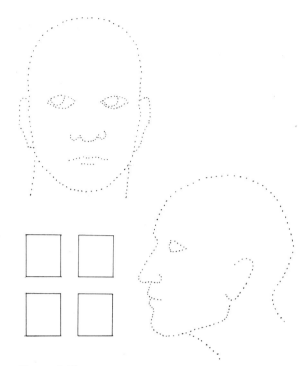

Figure 8–2b.

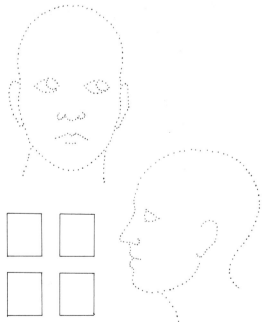

Figure 8–2c.

116

A section follows that includes "Period," "Show style," "Theatre," and "Lighting." Though not immediately applicable to the character being played, such information is essential when making choices about the makeup design in general.

Period

Creating makeup reflective of the period in which a show is set may require extensive research. A production of *Hamlet* staged in the 1700s would require quite a different design approach from one with a concept that places the action in the Victorian era. Beauty spots, face whiteners, a particular eye treatment or hair style can help transport the audience's imagination to another century.

Figure 8–3.
No one would mistake this character as "inappropriate" for the twentieth century.

Style

The style of a production can open wonderfully inventive avenues of makeup expression. The majority of productions are done in a realistic vein, but occasionally a show will be done in a manner that departs from what we expect to see in our everyday experience. Many shows, like *A Midsummer's Night Dream*, open the doors of stylistic imagination. Many children's scripts call for fanciful

Figure 8–4.
A stylistic concept can lead to exciting and novel makeup, particularly when done for children's shows as (c) and (d) illustrate.

a   b

c   d

characters, both human and animal. The makeup done for a show with a "cartoon" concept might benefit from a flat base and obvious line work to determine character. Approaching a production as a puppet show might require that "realistic" makeup be done with a suggestion of carved planes, or applied with more color intensity than normal. The opportunity to coordinate makeup design with costume or scenery design is obvious and can also be a very exciting approach.

It is very important in a stylized production that one person, or several working together *very* closely, design the makeup to avoid inconsistencies. Remember to let a type of line, a given color scheme, or even a particular choice of materials (such as cut paper, foils, or yarn) tie all of the designs together. Your makeup morgue can be very useful in finding pictures to get ideas from, be they toys, dolls, puppets, or illustrations from children's books.

Theatre

"Theatre" implies the physical relationship between the performer and the audience. Actors working on a large outdoor proscenium stage will require quite a different makeup application to play any given role than they would in a fifty-seat intimate arena theatre.

Figure 8–5.
Contrast is the essential difference between playing on a stage where the audience members are very close, and in a situation where they extend a great distance from the acting space. The makeup in (a) would read similar to (b) when viewed from a great distance.

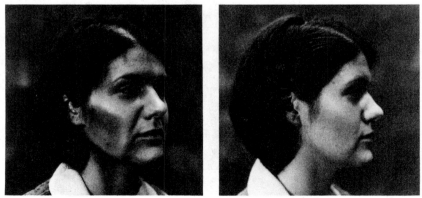

a   b

In a playing situation where the audience is as close as your classmates, "less is often more." Trying to go too far with an effect simply renders it obvious. Always experiment with the actors or actresses if possible, placing them on the stage and moving to various seats in the house to see what reads well and what needs to be toned down, emphasized, or eliminated. Whenever possible, use the lights that will be utilized for the actual production. Obviously, effects will look very different under stage worklights than under full theatrical lighting with its complexity of angles and colors.

Lighting

One cannot emphasize enough how influential lighting can be to successful or to disastrous makeup. It is important that the makeup designer be aware of both the lighting angles and gel colors when designing makeup. Some theatres suffer from a dearth of hanging positions, and they are often plagued with high angles that create deep shadows beneath the eyes, nose, and chin that must be corrected. Others have only low, frontal positions that tend to wash out the features and make the face appear flat. Greater contrast is often necessary in makeup to compensate for flatness and create dimension.

Figure 8–6.
In an acting area where lights are close to the performer, the makeup artist must combat harsh angles.

The color, as well as the angle, of light can have a tremendous effect on makeup. Generally, in a realistic production, lighting will be quite unsaturated in color, allowing a great deal of white light to fill the stage. This type of lighting does not change the color of the costumes, settings, or makeup appreciably. However, when gels that are more saturated in color are used, the light can have a measured effect on the pigmented colors on the stage. In fact, it can change them completely!

Discuss the colors with the lighting designer. It is also very helpful to procure some sample gels from him or her and place them in a light in the makeup room. This is the most efficient way to take the guesswork out of color choice.

As you can see in Figure 8–7, color in lighting differs somewhat from the color system used in mixing paints and makeup. This system of color was introduced in Chapter 4, but not elaborated upon at that time. Since the two systems of color work together on the stage in ways that can affect the makeup, their relationship needs to be explained a bit further.

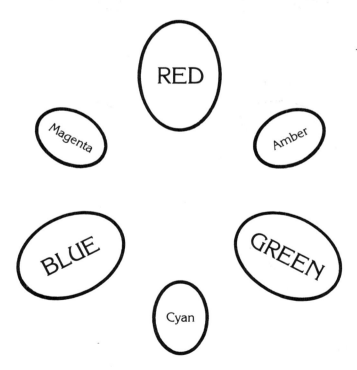

Figure 8–7.
This color wheel differs somewhat from the pigmented wheel in Figure 5–1, though both have primary and secondary colors.

Color in light also operates with primary and secondary colors, though they differ from the pigment system. Instead of the red, yellow, and blue that we are used to working with, blue, red, and green compose the primary colors. These primary colors, like the pigment system, can be combined to produce secondary colors as well. This is known as *addictive coloring*. Figures 8–8a, b, and c illustrate how adding two colors of light to the same acting area produces another color. Red and blue combine to produce magenta, while blue and green combine to create a blue-green color called cyan. Amber, however, is produced when a green light and a red light merge. When all the primary colors are aimed at the same area, pure white light results (see Figure 8–8d) since white is the result of all the colors in the spectrum.

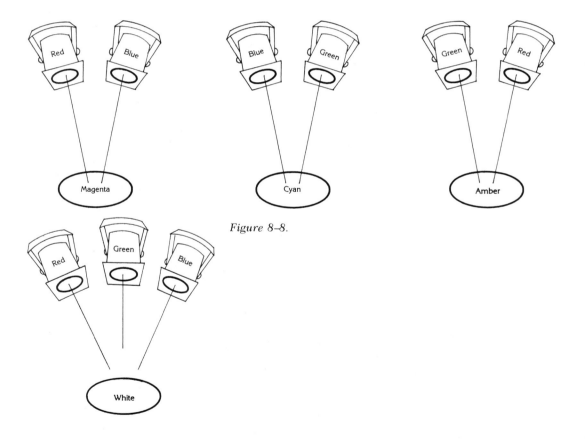

Figure 8–8.

Because the white light that is all around us contains all color, we enjoy a world rich in color, from the red of a dress to the green of a tree. When color in light is broken down to individual hues, however, its capacity is limited. A red light, for instance, can reflect only red, blue only blue. Figure 8–9 shows this principle. A red light aimed at a red book with white pages will turn the white pages red and make the red book look even redder. A white light, like the light all around us, will reflect the natural colors of the book. If, however, we were to shine a blue light on that same red book, the blue would not be able to show off the red, and it would simply turn it a dark gray or black. The white of the pages, however, would look blue. This principle, known as *subtractive color*, can apply directly to makeup. Since blue can reflect only blue, any makeup used in a night scene lit with strong blue gels will look gray or bluish. The lovely warm colors creating your complexion will simply not read. Blue or greenish shadows or highlights will consequently gray out under red lights as well.

Figure 8–9.

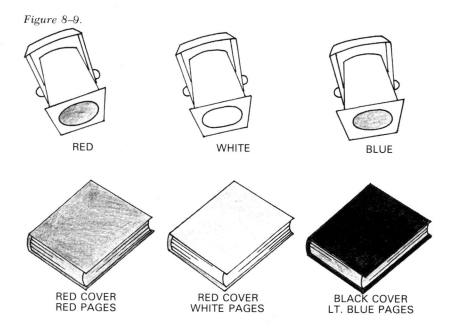

RED   WHITE   BLUE

RED COVER
RED PAGES

RED COVER
WHITE PAGES

BLACK COVER
LT. BLUE PAGES

Fortunately, very saturated colors in lighting are limited to special effects, or they are combined to create blazing white acting areas. It is not often that one will encounter major problems with subtractive color. Just to be safe, however, it is a good idea to test the colors you intend to use by placing them on your hand and looking at them under the lighting conditions for the production. It is ever so much easier to adjust your colors during rehearsals than to get ready for opening night and realize you look a little like a pile of soot. An essential prologue to character development with makeup consists of determining the artistic style of the show, the period in which it will be produced, the lighting that will be used, and the relationship between audience and performer. Together they help clarify some of the parameters of artistic choice: what colors should *not* be used, how heavy-handed one may be with cosmetics, to what extent prosthetics might be used, and whether an adherence to some degree of period is necessary. With these considerations in mind, one can confidently move on to the next section, which focuses on the role being played.

9

Preparing the Facial Map

When actors or actresses prepare for roles, they will, as a matter of course, consider the following items on the makeup map: age, temperament, nationality/race, health, profession, environment, climate, and distinguishing features. Analyzing the role in each of these areas provides knowledge and insights that all make contributions to the performer's choice of gestures, timing, attitude, voice, posture—and makeup. When the latter is skillfully designed to complement the others, a window is created that permits viewing deeply into the character, reflecting a full gamut of life experience. This makeup, however, must be balanced with the actor's physical and vocal development. "Age" is the one area where inconsistencies are obvious. It does little good, for instance, to effectively make up a young actor to look like an 80-year-old man if his gestures and voice read like that of a 50-year-old. A wise makeup artist will always watch the performer rather than rely on a script for descriptions. Performers who do their own makeup should get suggestions from the director and fellow performers when compiling an analysis from which makeup will be created.

125

Age

Aging the actor is the most common makeup problem. As a person ages, various changes occur depending on people's hereditary characteristics, their diet, exposure to the elements, muscle tone, and health. While one person may look much younger than how one expects a person of 60 to look, another might appear to be much older. Our society has expectations of persons in regard to how old they look—stereotypes that affect how we relate to them. One can be assured of the audience's sympathy if they create a frail, feeble old codger who looks one stop away from the cemetery. The old, senile woman in *The Effects of Gamma Rays on Man-in-the-Moon Marigolds* might be a good example of this, though she might only be 65. On the other hand, age must be worn quite differently on Halie, the older woman in Sam Shepard's *Buried Child*, though her age is probably about 65 as well. She exhibits a strength and character that would be confused by makeup that rendered her in a gaunt, feeble manner.

Study the script carefully and avoid assumptions as to age. Each person ages very differently.

The face of youth is smooth and uninterrupted by wrinkles. The complexion is usually very warm and colorful in appearance. The features tend to be soft and rounded, and the skin hugs the supporting muscles tightly. In our culture, it is often a time of incongruities, since there is such pressure to "grow up" quickly. On one hand, the adolescent face often wears a startling mask of makeup that makes her look much older, while on the other she still appears like a child putting on Mommy's makeup. John, the youngest son in *Lion in Winter*, is an excellent project in creating adolescence struggling with adulthood. The features of a college male would have to be softened appreciably, while creating the hint of a coming beard and the acned face of a gawky troubled youth.

By the late twenties, tiny wrinkles and gentle depressions begin to appear, and the overall complexion begins to lose its rich, light coloration. The thirties and early forties are perhaps the hardest to capture when doing makeup on the younger person, since changes are so subtle. The face of a person at this age has begun to

a   b   c

d   e   f

Figure 9–1.
The progression from a teenager to a senior citizen is a gradual one, as evidenced in these faces that reflect several decades.

change in coloration, losing its smooth flush and developing more texture. A darkness has often begun to develop along with small bags beneath the eyes. The tissue around the eyes, being thin, also begins to sport crow's feet and other tiny wrinkles. Creases are often evident where expressions have forced the skin to repeatedly fold on itself: the nasalabials, the forehead, and between the eyebrows. The substructure begins to soften, allowing a gradual relaxation of the jawline and the cheek area as well.

Beyond middle age, capillaries become more visible. The skin tone becomes more lax, and a mottled and unblended complexion becomes obvious. The jawline continues to soften as the flesh droops over it in various configurations such as jowls or a double chin. The flesh around the eyes thins and begins to depress as the skull form becomes more prominent. The flesh darkens in general, although some people, because of poor circulation, tend to become paler.

As one moves into old age, the skin becomes thin and almost translucent. The nose begins to droop, and the cheek and chin bones seem to protrude. In very old people, the whites of the eyes often yellow, and the lower eyelid, because of relaxing muscles, appears as a pink rim. The eyeballs seem to sink somewhat as the relief of the bony skull becomes more prominent. In addition, veins, age spots, and discolored patches add color and richness to the complexion.

Temperament

Aging is an obvious process of structural and color change that we have little control over. People's temperaments, on the other hand, are often etched in the lines and angles of their faces as residues of the expressions they make in response to their moods or feelings throughout their lifetime. Perhaps you can remember your mother admonishing your frowns with the words, "If you aren't careful, your face will freeze in that position!" Well, to some degree, she was right. If one continually draws the facial muscles into the same position, creases in the skin will eventually develop. People who continually knit their eyebrows in anger, pushing the flexible skin between them into vertical creases, may find these furrows remain even when they are smiling.

Certainly people's temperaments can be shown in lines, wrinkles, and the angles of their face, as we learned from looking at and drawing cartoons. Color may be used to indicate temperament in some situations. Persons with a loud, quick temper may have broken blood vessels on the surface of their skin, which will render the complexion a reddish hue. Forlorn, pining individuals may have a pale, lifeless color to their skin.

Sculpting the shape of the features in general may lend a sense of temperament. Squaring off the features and making them more prominent would help convey a character who is burly and throws his or her weight around, while a softer, heart-shaped face with delicate features might better support a weaker nature. A wishy-washy personality might be reinforced by downplaying any salient features. A shapeless nose, receding chin, and weak cheek bones might be appropriate.

Profession

Some early physiognomists believed that no matter how delicate a man's profession, it required the use of various muscles that would map out the man's line of work. They held that the carpenter developed tiny lines about the eyes from squinting at the measuring stick, the glass-blower had exaggerated cheek muscles, and so on. No proof was ever found for this short-lived thesis, although it is obvious that *some* professions can leave physical evidence useful to the makeup artist.

Characters engaged in their work are often easiest to define with makeup. Yank, the furnace stoker in *The Hairy Ape*, would be quite easy to make up. A soot-covered face, ruddy from the heat would be appropriate. Sweat, dripping from damp, matted hair might streak across the features, intensifying the effects of the heat. Bruises, scratches, band-aids, or burns might lend testimony to a boxer, wrestler, firefighter, or dog catcher, while deeply tanned faces (with a pale forehead where the cap protected it) might be appropriate for farmers or other outdoor laborers. Miners retain a somewhat sooty look since even after washing particles of coal remain imbedded in the skin; for them, a gray, dusty look might be appropriate.

Movies and television have conditioned us to relate to many professions in a stereotypic manner. The prostitute generally has bleached hair and gobs of makeup, while the harried housewife contends with a facial pack and curlers. The cleaning lady is generally pictured with a frumpy expression, unkempt hair, no makeup, and well-earned bags beneath her eyes. The wino, of course, has a three-day growth of beard, disheveled hair, and red eyes. Though these images may immediately spring to our minds, it is not always wise to utilize them, as they tend to flatten out and limit most characterizations. Consider how important the profession is to the role and what the character is trying to say with it before making final conclusions as to makeup choices.

Environment

There is little doubt that we are all, in some ways, a reflection of our past or present environment. Sometimes, in the case of extreme living conditions, the physical evidence is clear. In other situations, our environment has affected us psychologically, and the results lie more in expressions and subtle indications.

A very obvious clue to one's immediate environment may show in the state of cleanliness. People living in Appalachian poverty, migrant camps, ghettos, some foreign countries, and the streets of many large cities may have dirty bodies and hair as evidence of neglect and lack of hygiene. Only in the last century, even in "civilized" nations blessed with indoor plumbing and advertising, has personal hygiene been a priority at all. Though one would hardly choose to emphasize the point, most of the characters in Shakespeare's plays undoubtedly washed their hair but a few times a year, rarely bathed, wore clothes for weeks at a time before changing them, and probably hosted quite a variety of tiny multilegged critters!

Before institutional reform, squalid conditions prevailed in jails, orphanages, mental wards, and hospitals. Orphans, prisoners, the senile, and retarded were often kept in filthy habitats. Matted hair, dirty skin, sores, and abrasions abounded. Though such images make wonderful inspiration for characters, some concessions have to be made as a rule to align with what contemporary standards dictate. If the characters in *Marat Sade* or *Man of La Mancha* truly reflected their period environment, no audience member could enjoy the production!

The cultural, religious, or social customs evident in one's environment may also be reflected in the makeup, as groups reject the standards promoted in fashion magazines and the media. Those exposed to an Amish environment, for instance, would appear to wear no makeup. The women would arrange their hair in a natural

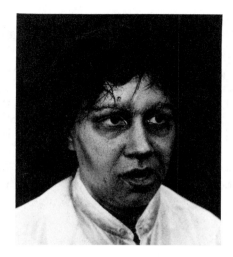

Figure 9–2.
This makeup effectively helps portray an abused character in a mental ward.

style, while the men would evidence a simple cut and beards for those who were married.

The hippies of the sixties, who chose to live a lifestyle apart from general society, would certainly reflect their environment as well: a return to the natural, though somewhat unkempt, appearance.

The product of environmental factors often overlaps into temperament. A kid growing up in a tough street atmosphere may show a maturity in advance of his years—either a hardened look or the dazed, burned-out look of an addict. On the other hand, he might look fearful, broken in spirit, and abused. These factors must be handled more delicately than the obvious elements of dirt and bruises, unkempt hair, and missing teeth. In either case, however, it is important that the makeup designer work closely with the costume designer. Both must work for the same "look" and therefore have identical feelings about the character being analyzed.

Climate

The contrast between the complexions of a safari guide and a business executive would be quite dramatic. One probably spends many hours in the sun, while the second flourishes under the fluorescent glow of an office lamp.

The actual climate to which a character is exposed is not nearly so important as our impression of what that climate implies. Most of us tend to think of England as a cool, damp country where sunshine is a rare occurrence. So, while the sun does indeed shine and many Britons are indeed tan, an audience would undoubtedly *expect* to see a proper British gentleman with a pale complexion. By the same token, the audience might be confused if a play set in the tropics had only characters of a ghostly complexion populating it.

Though admittedly climate is a secondary consideration to health and nationality, it can sometimes be very effective in helping to separate characters, enrich a character's background, and lend a sense of season and locale.

a

b

c

d

e

Figure 9–3.
Many nationalities and races possess unique characteristics in contour and coloring that often make them readily identifiable.

Race/Nationality

The race or nationality of a character is often an important element that affects how we perceive him or her in the context of the script. Since we expect Othello the Moor to be dark, the entire play would alter in power and meaning if he strode onto the stage with fair complexion and red hair. The theme of a play like *Indians* would be shattered if Chief Joseph looked Italian, and making Sherlock Holmes up to look Oriental would certainly put a different slant on that production as well. In productions such as these, where the audience has a preconceived notion of the character's race or nation of origin, it is usually unwise to depart from them since the play may very well be weakened by an innovative interpretation.

In many cases, however, the race or nationality of a particular character is not integral to the movement of the plot and is probably not even mentioned. In that case, one may either ignore this section entirely or assign a particular race or nationality to that role, if in doing so, the performer's portrayal will somehow be strengthened.

Health

Hippocrates said that a man's face was the greatest diagnostic tool available in determining his health. We need not always know someone to be able to tell if he or she is feeling dreadful or in the pink.

Color is perhaps the most obvious clue to one's health. When one is very ill, the entire complexion seems drained, leaving it with a definite pallor. A yellowish or even yellow-green tint *can* be quite effective when applied as a stipple over other colors, or as a thin base. (Be cautious, however, or the "victim" will look like a grade B monster.) A person in very bad health will have eyes tinged with a reddish hue. The mouth will droop at the corners, with the eyelids following suit. The features tend to sharpen, the eye sockets deepen, and the cheeks appear more hollow as well.

There are certainly departures from this format depending upon the illness, and symptoms should be researched. In some cases, the face will bloat, turn red, yellow, or variegated. Sores, blotches, and skin eruptions of every conceivable type are possible, and they may add a great deal to the believability of various illnesses.

Special Features

Some characters have "built-in" requirements that are so established in the minds of the audience members that to ignore or change them might weaken the roles. Can you imagine Falstaff as a 97-pound weakling? Fagin with a set of coiffured curls? Or Cyrano with a pug nose? And what would the hunchback of Notre Dame be without his hunch? It can be risky to alter the image that resides in the memory and imagination of the audience member.

Sometimes special features may be added to a role to lend more personality. A scar, a moustache, a broken nose, or a bald pate are examples. Frequently such a special touch is all that is needed to render the role "just right," in that it flatters not only the performer wearing it, but the other cast members as well.

Before moving on to the last section of the facial map, check each of the previous items to make certain that you have gleaned as much information from the script, performer, and director as possible. Each is a potential avenue of communication between the performer and the audience. Some characters who seem poorly sketched in the script may take on an exciting degree of personality when supplied with a "profession" or "state of health" by a creative actor or director. Certainly the more information the makeup artist has, the better, as we shall see as we move on to the final section of the analysis page of the makeup map.

There are no two faces exactly alike. Compare features whenever even a few people gather, and you will be amazed at the diversity of shapes, sizes, and colorings. The human face is marvelously flexible, with an arrangement of muscles that allow us to alter it in thousands of expressive ways. Applying makeup can emphasize, extend, or completely alter the structure and expression of

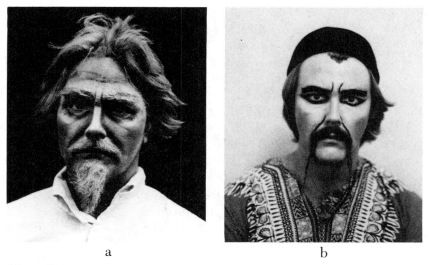

a   b

Figure 9–4.
With makeup, one can accentuate or change human features. This actor has utilized cosmetics to completely alter his face for two quite different roles.

the face to an even greater degree. There is not a feature on the face that cannot be modified in wonderful ways.

The eyebrows can be plucked, thickened, or eliminated altogether with wax, while the eyes can be colored, shaped with shading, or turned into Oriental configurations (see Chapter 12).

The mouth can easily be altered in shape with cosmetics, or changed by adding strips of foam inside the mouth and adhering them with dental adhesives. (Don't wait until final rehearsal to try this, however, as articulation can be somewhat impaired and one may need practice talking!)

Cheeks can be puffed out with "plumpers" of foam or modified with simple shading. Foam latex prosthetics are often utilized in altering the cheek and the adjacent jaw into sagging jowls.

The nose is wonderfully flexible. With proper shading, or the addition of wax or foam pieces, it can seemingly shrink or actually grow in length and size.

The forehead is often altered with shading and highlight as well. Extending the hairline by plucking, shaving, or soaping will create a "higher" look, while adding to the hair line and eyebrows with crepe hair will effectively "shorten" the forehead.

A popular sixties song, "Hair," from the famous musical of the same name went on for stanzas about the wonders of this most flexible feature. No other feature so quickly conveys not only age, but social status, politics, and periods as well. It can be cut, curled, braided, frizzed, teased, waxed, sprayed, singed, and painted, changing the nature of the wearer, the shape of the face, and lending an array of different personalities. Add facial hair such as eyebrows, moustaches, and beards, and one has endless possibilities for change.

All of the facial features are listed in the final section of the analysis sheet. One needs to consider how to best convey age, temperament, health, climate, and the like through each feature in the designing of appropriate makeup.

Having one's makeup morgue handy is almost a necessity in this process, as one can reap many ideas by making composites of the pictures. Taking one feature at a time, consider all of the information about the character, and find visuals in your morgue that most exemplify each.

Studying photographs of people in the same age bracket as the character to be played will help determine what lines, folds, and wrinkles, as well as facial texture might be appropriate. Ideas to

Figure 9–5.
Hair styles, including facial hair, can not only completely change appearance, but can establish period, personality, and social status.

a　　　　　　　　　　b　　　　　　　　　　c

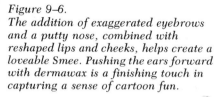

Figure 9–6.
The addition of exaggerated eyebrows and a putty nose, combined with reshaped lips and cheeks, helps create a loveable Smee. Pushing the ears forward with dermawax is a finishing touch in capturing a sense of cartoon fun.

convey the temperament, particularly through the eyes and mouth, can be found by locating pictures of people who seem to convey this same attitude. Your section on races and nationalities should indicate not only coloring and structural differences, but perhaps culturally induced facial decorations such as eye treatments, scarring, or face painting. Variations in climate and their effect on the features and complexion can be taken from the "complexions" section of the morgue. One's environment can be indicated with dirt and bruises, high fashion makeup, or any number of things. For appropriate applications, again check your file. Magazines, such as *National Geographic*, are excellent sources for this type of research. Looking through these visuals may also give you ideas for a special or distinguishing feature that you might not have considered otherwise, be it a cauliflower ear, a swollen lip, or a fancy waxed moustache.

Once you have compiled numerous pictures that will be helpful in creating the proper characterization, move on to the second page of the analysis, which is the actual facial map. This is essentially a worksheet for drawings and notes. When complete, the map can be placed on the performer's mirror, along with any reference pictures, providing all the necessary information one needs for actually applying the makeup.

10

Constructing
the Facial Map

Making Words
into Pictures

The actual facial map may come in one of several forms, as we shall soon see. In order to be useful, however, a makeup map, regardless of its format, should include the following items: front and side views of the male or female head, an abundance of space for writing notes to supplement the actual drawing, and a place to indicate which colors should be used.

The maps in Figures 8–2a and b provide these needs. The heads are both indicated with dots so that the shape can be easily altered to accommodate the individual features of any actor or actress. Though this approach is certainly adequate, it is far better to use the contour portraits of the performer suggested in the chapter on line, or trace the performer's face from a photograph. By working from the exact facial configuration of the actor or actress, the original features are clear, making it a simple matter to evaluate methods and degrees of change necessary or possible to create particular effects. It will do little good to sketch lovely round eyes on the facial map when the actress has naturally squinty ones.

The four boxes in the lower left corner of these maps are for color swatches. One may use crayon, pastel, colored pencil, or actual makeup to indicate the colors that are to be used in composing the complexion range. The highlight, transitional, and shading color, as well as the primary stipple, should be indicated. Additional boxes may be drawn when more colors are planned. It is imperative to include this color information so that the complexion colors can be matched with consistency each night of the performance.

Figure 10–1a.

Figure 10–1b.

Filling out this page with accuracy is obviously quite important. Not only must all the information collected on the analysis page be translated into visual form, it must be done in such a way as to avoid any confusion when applying the actual makeup. Some performers use more than one map, one for each application of a separate color. Others use one map for basic structuring with shading and a transparent overlay for wrinkle work when doing old age. Figure 10–2a shows a map that simply designates with line which areas of the face correspond with the color swatches. Figure 10–3a uses shaded areas to designate each different color. This type of approach provides a simple guide to facial division and color application. The map can be lightly transferred with an eyebrow pencil and "filled in."

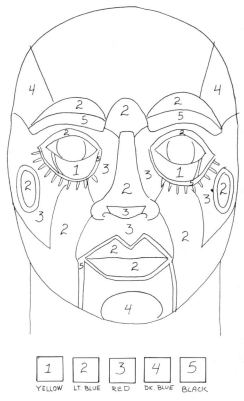

Figure 10–2a.

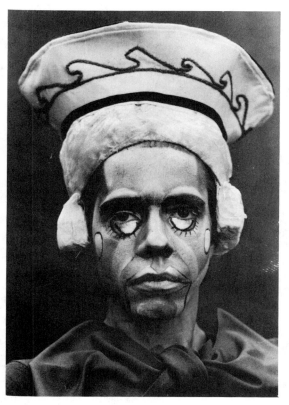

Figure 10–2b.

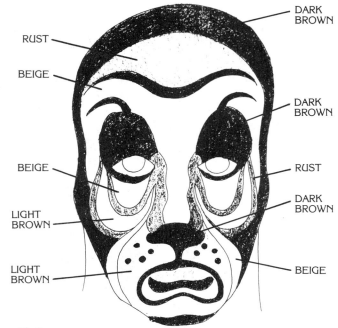

RUST

DARK
BROWN

BEIGE

DARK
BROWN

BEIGE

RUST

LIGHT
BROWN

DARK
BROWN

LIGHT
BROWN

BEIGE

Figure 10–3a.

Figure 10–3b.

Figure 10–4.
Placing visuals in an acetate sleeve protects them from damage. In addition, notes can be written in grease pencil on the plastic, saving the picture.

While this type of map is useful for stylized work or for realistic applications of little complexity, most makeup applications will benefit far more if a map is prepared to include the actual shading of the colors. Since it is difficult to gauge true relationships when working on white paper, tinted or colored stock is recommended. The makeup maps that conclude this chapter were all done on colored paper so that both highlights and shadows could be worked out for dimensional accuracy and correct placement. Color compatibility can also be judged on this type of a visual.

As you have undoubtedly gathered, a great deal of visual information is conveyed by the properly composed facial map. Although it takes time to do a proper analysis of the character being played, and even more time to render the actual facial map, the rewards are reaped immediately. Performers are not only able to apply makeup with ease, having made all the important decisions regarding the application beforehand, but they are assured of a makeup that will effectively reflect the very essence of the role being played.

The following pages include a variety of characters from well known scripts. Before and after pictures of the performers are provided as well as the facial maps and analysis sheets done in preparation for the actual application.

PRODUCTION *Beggar's Opera*   DATE *10-16*
CHARACTER *Highwayman*   PERFORMER *Brian*
PERIOD *1830*
SHOW STYLE *"Overdone" Realism—Earthy Characters*
THEATRE *Small Proscenium House*
LIGHTING *Lots of Colors, Angles, Special Effects*
AGE *22*
TEMPERAMENT *Nasty, Crude, Loud*
NATIONALITY/RACE *Caucasian — British Perhaps*
HEALTH *Good*
PROFESSION *Rowdy, Thief, Drunk*
ENVIRONMENT *Dirty*
CLIMATE *Warm Days — Cool Nights*
DISTINGUISHING FEATURES
EYES/EYEBROWS *Hard, Piercing —Dark around eye,*
MOUTH *Bad Teeth, Stained, Chipped*   *Angled Brow*
CHEEKS *Angular, a bit sunken*
NOSE *Crooked from fighting*
CHIN/JAW *Cleft, Squared*
FOREHEAD *Flat, angled at temple*
HAIR *Grease-coated, Tangled*
OTHER *Should have repulsive look—*

  scars, acne, dirt

Figure 10–5a.

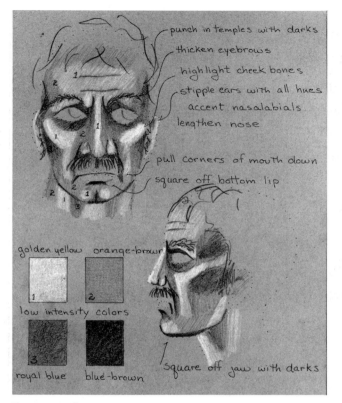

punch in temples with darks

thicken eyebrows

highlight cheek bones

stipple ears with all hues

accent nasalabials

lengthen nose

pull corners of mouth down

square off bottom lip

golden yellow   orange-brown

low intensity colors

royal blue   blue-brown

square off jaw with darks

Figure 10–5b.

Figure 10–5c.

Figure 10–5d.

PRODUCTION: Alice in Wonderland   DATE:

CHARACTER: Queen of Hearts   PERFORMER: DOROTHY

PERIOD: a 19th century flavor, very "fairy tale" in quality

SHOW STYLE: stylized - cartoon - obviously flat and painted

THEATRE: small arena

LIGHTING: colorful, harsh, strong

AGE: "older"

TEMPERAMENT: nasty, stern, cool, aloof, haughty

NATIONALITY/RACE:

HEALTH: good

PROFESSION: ruling subjects, complaining

ENVIRONMENT: flat, stylized "Wonderland"

CLIMATE: warm

DISTINGUISHING FEATURES: must wear a "heart" on her face

EYES/EYEBROWS: sharp, angles brows, vertical creases, small, beady

MOUTH: sharp, pointed, pulled down

CHEEKS: obvious dimension on cheeks, sharp, high

NOSE: thin, sharp, well-defined

CHIN/JAW: hard, distinct jowel

FOREHEAD: short, narrow

HAIR: hard, fake style

COMMENTS: Features should be defined and distinct to create the stylized look. The color range should be pink, rose and burgundy, creating a warm, cupid-like coloring similar to a china doll.

Figure 10–6a.

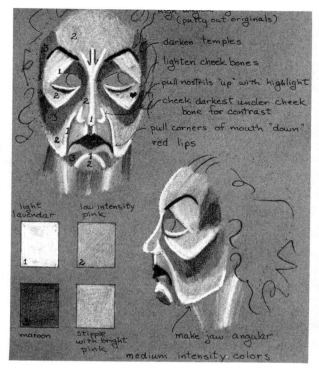

High light (putty out originals)
darken temples
lighten cheek bones
pull nostrils "up" with highlight
cheek darkest under cheek bone for contrast
pull corners of mouth "down"
red lips

light lavender
low intensity pink
maroon
stipple with bright pink
medium intensity colors
make jaw angular

Figure 10–6b.

Figure 10–6c.

Figure 10–6d.

PRODUCTION: Look Homeward Angel   DATE:

CHARACTER: Eliza   PERFORMER: Nikki

PERIOD: 1920s

SHOW STYLE: very realistic

THEATRE: arena thrust

LIGHTING: soft, even with unsaturated gels in pinks and blues

AGE: later 40s

TEMPERAMENT: strong, firm, selfish, undaunted

NATIONALITY/RACE: caucasian

HEALTH: good

PROFESSION: runs a boarding house

ENVIRONMENT: active, demanding

CLIMATE: warm summer

DISTINGUISHING FEATURES:

EYES/EYEBROWS: stern, unruly brows, slightly aged and tired with perhaps
darkening circles

MOUTH: firm, almost severe

CHEEKS: angled, with prominent cheekbones

NOSE: well-defined with lines running vertically between brows

CHIN/JAW: defined, rigid, slight droop in nasalabial

FOREHEAD: lined, high

HAIR: short and dark, with grey touches in a simple "homemade" style

COMMENTS: The complexion should have a "powdered and rouged" quality that
moves her away from a warm, inviting, natural look. The mouth must be thinned
and strengthened. All soft, youthful contours should be shaped in a more angular
fashion.

Figure 10–7a.

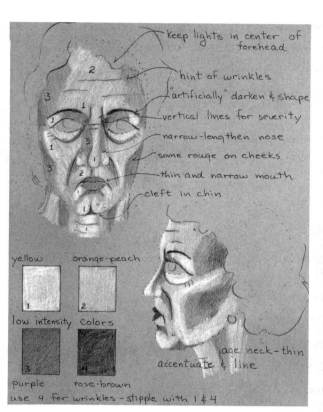

keep lights in center of forehead

hint of wrinkles

"artificially" darken & shape

vertical lines for severity

narrow-lengthen nose

some rouge on cheeks

thin and narrow mouth

cleft in chin

yellow — orange-peach

low intensity Colors

purple — rose-brown

use 4 for wrinkles - stipple with 1 & 4

age neck - thin
accentuate & line

Figure 10–7b.

Figure 10–7c.

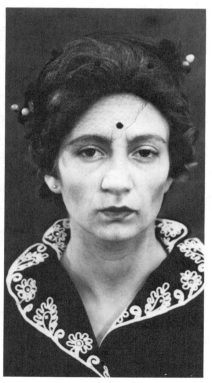

Figure 10–7d.

149

PRODUCTION: Macbeth   DATE:

CHARACTER: witch   PERFORMER: Annette

PERIOD: 1500-1600

SHOW STYLE: fragmented realism

THEATRE: long-play outdoor stage

LIGHTING: stylized in witch scenes - fog, shafts of color, etc.

AGE: ageless, but generally old

TEMPERAMENT: aloof, wise, mysterious, almost sinister

NATIONALITY/RACE:

HEALTH: no quality of health as humans know it

PROFESSION: spirit

ENVIRONMENT: unfriendly, unearthly, mystical

CLIMATE: cold

DISTINGUISHING FEATURES:

EYES/EYEBROWS: should be striking with an "other world" feel without being bizarre

MOUTH: well defined, turned down sternly, upper lip is curved like a cats

CHEEKS: well defined, high, with sunken hollows

NOSE: elongated and distinctly angular

CHIN/JAW: hard with chin accentuated

FOREHEAD: low, dark temples, shaped and lined

HAIR: wild, close around face

COMMENTS: Face should have a fearful look, while remaining soft enough to avoid totally stylized look. The color range should be in the blue-grey, rose-grey range, with deep purples as shadowing. A light blue-grey stipple will add texture as well as punch up the prominent features.

Figure 10–8a.

Figure 10–8b.

shaggy, matted hair

clear depressions on forehead

angle eyebrows sharply

accent pads

hollow cheeks deeply

square nose off at bottom

create new lip line

warm lavendar dusty rose

medium-high intensity colors

blue-purple purple

create skeletal effect on neck

use 4 for deep wrinkles-stipple with 2 & 4

Figure 10–8c.

Figure 10–8d.

151

PRODUCTION: Man of LaMancha   DATE:

CHARACTER: Aldonza   PERFORMER: Jennifer

PERIOD: inquisition

SHOW STYLE: bold, overdone - abstract lighting and sets

THEATRE: small proscenium with balcony

LIGHTING: lots of color - many shadows and dark areas

AGE: 28

TEMPERAMENT: hardened by the world - not in touch with herself - playing the survival game

NATIONALITY/RACE: Spanish

HEALTH: good to fair - probably has social disease - doesn't take care of herrself

PROFESSION: bar wench, prostitute, prisoner

ENVIRONMENT: squalid, crowded, abusive

CLIMATE: hot

DISTINGUISHING FEATURES:

EYES/EYEBROWS: dark, angular eyebrows, - moody, dark, piercing eyes

MOUTH: pouting, sensual, hard

CHEEKS: angular and sunken

NOSE: sharp but shapely

CHIN/JAW: angular, hard

FOREHEAD: flat

HAIR: unkempt with sense that it might have been lovely once

COMMENTS: A scar on her cheek, pox marks and dirt would be appropriate. Her color should be pale and evoke a fraility, while the shape suggests strength. Dark hair and eyes should lend Spanish quality

Figure 10–9a.

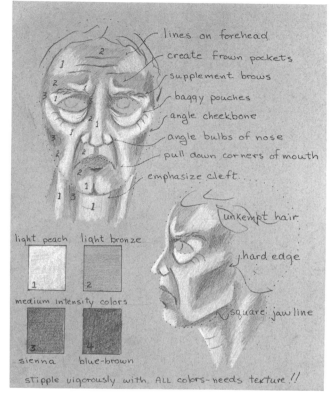

lines on forehead
create frown pockets
supplement brows
baggy pouches
angle cheekbone
angle bulbs of nose
pull down corners of mouth
emphasize cleft....

unkempt hair

hard edge

square jawline

light peach   light bronze

1   2

medium intensity colors

3   4

sienna   blue-brown

stipple vigorously with ALL colors-needs texture !!

Figure 10–9b.

Figure 10–9c.

Figure 10–9d.

PRODUCTION: A Christmas Carol   DATE:

CHARACTER: Scrooge   PERFORMER: Doug

PERIOD: late 19th century

SHOW STYLE: realism with Disney quality

THEATRE: large proscenium house

LIGHTING: softly sculpted with warm washes - cool in dream scenes

AGE: 75

TEMPERAMENT: cranky, rude, selfish

NATIONALITY/RACE: English

HEALTH: only fair

PROFESSION: businessman - miser

ENVIRONMENT: (industrial revolution) sterile, pressured

CLIMATE: cold, damp, foggy, miserable

DISTINGUISHING FEATURES:

EYES/EYEBROWS: thick, angular brows, deep piercing eyes set in

MOUTH: firm, thin, tight - lines from pursing lips, pulled downward

CHEEKS: angular, hollow, prominent nasalabials

NOSE: hard, long, thin

CHIN/JAW: hard, square, lean

FOREHEAD: lined with hollow temples

HAIR: thinning, grey, rather long

COMMENTS: age spots and lots of stipple texturing are appropriate

Figure 10–10a.

Figure 10–10c.

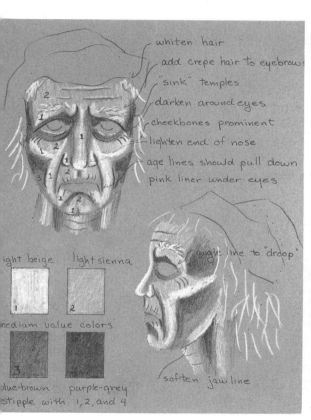

whiten hair
add crepe hair to eyebrows
"sink" temples
darken around eyes
cheekbones prominent
lighten end of nose
age lines should pull down
pink liner under eyes

light beige   light sienna

1   2

medium value colors

3   4

blue-brown   purple-grey
stipple with 1, 2, and 4

"angle line to 'droop'"

soften jawline

Figure 10–10b.

Figure 10–10d.

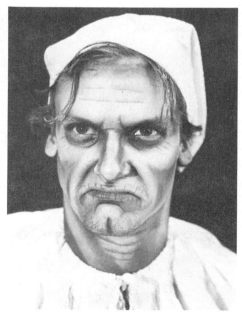

155

PRODUCTION: A Midsummer's Night Dream   DATE:

CHARACTER: Puck   PERFORMER: Lynn

PERIOD: Elizabethan - forest - somewhat fantasy oriented

SHOW STYLE: concept is "beds" - valentine idea

THEATRE: arena thrust

LIGHTING: shafts of light - cool colors - moody

AGE: sixteen going on ageless

TEMPERAMENT: jealous, self-centered, quick, in love with Oberon

NATIONALITY/RACE: forest creature, sense of animal, fairy quality

HEALTH: excellent

PROFESSION: prankster

ENVIRONMENT: forest - with feel of tawdry carnival side show

CLIMATE: dark, moist

DISTINGUISHING FEATURES: none

EYES/EYEBROWS: bright, appealing, merry, full of fire

MOUTH: small and pouting, but sensuous

CHEEKS: round and friendly

NOSE: pug, animal-like

CHIN/JAW: round

FOREHEAD: round, small

HAIR: curls, loose and free, unkempt look

COMMENTS: The makeup must not only create a youthful, sprite-like character, but most do it in such a way as to appear very much a part of the forest. The eyes and upper lip should be treated as that of a cat-like creature.

Figure 10–11a.

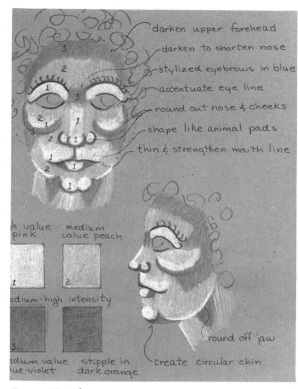

darken upper forehead
darken to shorten nose
stylized eyebrows in blue
accentuate eye line
round out nose & cheeks
shape like animal pads
thin & strengthen mouth line

h value pink
medium value peach

edium-high intensity

edium value lue-violet
stipple in dark orange

round off jaw
create circular chin

Figure 10–11b.

Figure 10–11c.

Figure 10–11d.

157

11

Sources

Like a drowning animal, the yak and horsehair wig, askew with springs and strings, floated in a bucket of gasoline. The actor, who only moments ago had been dipping the moppet to clean it, had abruptly abandoned the project to turn down a small odorous stove over which a block of hard mascara oozed liquid from the heat and deposited a sooty smoke on the mirror. From nails sticking from the mirror's frame dangled silk gauze and papier maché prosthetics, a bulbous nose, and a grease-soaked set of jowls. Porcelain tins marched along a wall, protecting their ingredients of lard-based greasepaints from spoilage. Burned cork, black varnish for teeth, leather drawing stumps, and assorted brushes littered the counter. A large lambswool puff to absorb oils lay in a cigar box along with cork shavings and sticking plaster, used to fill the spaces in ill-fitting wigs. The slightly rancid smell of Crisco, a staple for removing makeup, could be sensed among the other heavy odors.

Entering a makeup room of a theatre in the first decade of this century would undoubtedly have reminded one of Merlin's laboratory or a torture chamber of medieval past! One might surmise that the rabbit's foot carried by a performer of this time was not simply to dab excess oils and perspiration from his brow!

Prior to 1873, an actor had little choice in terms of makeup. Most concocted their own recipes using pork fat as a base. Colored powders were added to this sticky substance to create a variety of

159

base complexions, hence the term "ham" actor. Little more than a century ago, Ludwig Leichner, a German opera star and chemist, formulated the first commercially available greasepaint, starting a tradition of fine theatre cosmetics. Unlike many cosmetics of this time, Leichner's products were chemically safe. Many products, available from the local barber, druggist, or medicine man were composed of arsenics, mercury, and a host of other lethal poisons which caused baldness, paralysis, permanent scarring, or even death. Needless to say, acting was a risky profession at this time. It is rumored that one little lady in New York advertised greasepaint for the actor that was so safe, she would bite off a chunk and eat it. History does not record whether or not she lived long enough to collect social security!

It was not only the cosmetics, but the application of them that was an absolute horror at the turn of the century. Makeup manuals urged the actor to compensate for the unnatural illumination created by footlights by using a crude, thick application ornamented with illogical colorings. These techniques were adopted for the silent films, since a thick application was necessary to keep blood vessels, freckles, and blemishes from showing up black on the film. The mask of makeup sometimes included putties, which were applied so thickly that wrinkles could simply be scratched into the surface for old age!

Better film processes and improved lighting demanded a change in makeup, as the "talkies" entered the scene. A young perukier, who had traveled to America some years before with the Moscow Art Theatre and became involved with the new American film-making industry, revolutionized makeup application almost overnight. Max Factor was responsible for inventing a type of makeup that adopted "panchromatic" for its name after the film type for which it was originally designed.

This first improvement led to another and another, until by 1930 commercially manufactured stage and film makeups were a rapidly expanding industry with international distribution. Television makeup was added to the available line in 1932 when Factor developed the first makeup for use with television production. Lee, Lockwood, Leichner, Factor, and Stein, all leaders in the field, began altering their line of offerings from the heavy powders and greasepaints so popular only a decade before, to lighter, more diverse products. A watercolor makeup appeared, along with transparent powders, cream paints which left a matte finish, colored creams in jars, and in 1937 a dry cake makeup that was applied with a damp sponge. This makeup, called "pancake," marked another leap forward in application. When it made its debut in a 1939 film, the critics, in an unprecedented move, singled out the makeup for a rave review! Its popularity caught on so quickly that women began buying it for street makeup!

Despite the changes in two-dimensional cosmetics, the most rapid advancements were occurring with three-dimensional buildups. Collodion, poured gelatin, putty, and wax, once the staples of the professional world, were quickly abandoned for new methods and materials that promised lighter, more flexible prosthetics. Oddly enough, the medical field spawned this movement, rather than actors or artists. New plastics and foams were being devised for rebuilding the limbs and faces of returning war veterans. The excellent results in the operating room prompted their adoption by the world of entertainment. The first prosthetic for cinematic use appeared in 1939. Jack Dawn, a brilliant sculptor and makeup artist, created the lion for *The Wizard of Oz* with foam latex.

The thirties also saw the unionization of makeup artists in 1937. By 1940, makeup directors were hired for television and the legitimate theatre as well, providing a new standardization and level of quality.

The 1950s saw a rapid acceleration in the growth of television, as well as many changes in film techniques. The advent of the color process in both fields was added incentive to develop new products. The need for television makeup was at its peak, since every inch of exposed flesh had to be covered. Technical improvements today dictate that almost no makeup be used, causing a great revision in application only in the last decade.

Today's makeup artist draws on decades of change—new, improved cosmetics and space-age materials. Resins, rubbers, plastics, modern adhesives, and pigments are combined to create unlimited possibilities. Fifty years ago, an audience member was entranced with makeup that made an actor look like a monster, an oldster, or an animal, but he was always aware that an actor lurked beneath the buildups. Today, the effects that can be obtained with new materials are so convincing, we *believe* that Dustin Hoffman had really aged seventy years during the course of *Little Big Man*. We must remind ourselves that such creatures as King Kong and lovable ET are in fact *not* real!

There are many manufacturers of theatrical makeup today, most offering a broad range of products to accommodate film, television, and theatre. In addition, many items such as lipsticks, rouges, powder, liners, makeup removers, and blemish creams, are available on the shelves of a local drug or dime store, manufactured by a commercial firm.

Some of the most well known manufacturers of cosmetics for the stage and screen include the following:

BOB KELLY
151 West 46th Street, New York, N.Y. 10036

Kelly was known for his wig-making company long before he founded his own cosmetic company in 1960. In that short time, his products have become popular all over the US, Canada, and abroad. Kelly is noted for his humorous demonstrations on makeup applications.

LEICHNER PRODUCTS
559 11th Street, New York, N.Y. 10036

The excellence of these pure nonallergenic cosmetics, made by one of the oldest companies, has given them an excellent reputation the world over.

MAX FACTOR
1655 N. McCadden Place, Hollywood, Cal. 90028

Max Factor Sr. has been responsible for a great many innovations in theatrical and screen makeup for a period spanning half a century. Factor's extensive line not only caters to the entertainment world, but encompasses the fashion world as well. The Factor industry is massive, employing more than 8,000 people in 120 countries and producing hundreds of fine products known the world over.

KRYOLAN
745 Polk Street, San Francisco, Cal. 94109
 Also known as Kryolan Brandel, this company is one of the most progressive and fastest growing in the world today. It offers many fine quality products not manufactured by anyone else.

BEN NYE
11571 Santa Monica Boulevard, Los Angeles, Cal. 90025
 Nye Sr. was originally a commercial artist who eventually became the director of makeup for 20th Century Fox Productions, a position he held for 23 years. While there, he was responsible for many innovations, including the first cosmetics especially formulated for blacks. His high-quality products reflect an artist who is familiar with the needs of this field.

MEHRON INC.
250 West 40th Street, New York, N.Y. 10018
 This company, in business since 1927, offers an extensive array of reasonably priced products that are of excellent quality.

 One may write to these companies for a list of products and price sheets. However, you may save a little time and a few stamps by writing to one of the following theatre supply houses. Each carries several lines of makeup and can provide you with a list of products currently on the market. *Theatre Crafts* magazine publishes a national directory annually that lists dozens more. You may purchase a copy of this catalogue by writing to *Theatre Crafts*, 33 East Minor Street, Emmaus, Pa. 18049.

ALCONE CO. INCORPORATED
Paramount Theatrical Supplies
575 8th Avenue
New York, N.Y. 10018

CABARET COSTUME
1302 Kingsdale Avenue
Redondo Beach, Cal. 90277

CALIFORNIA THEATRE SUPPLY
747 Polk Street
San Francisco, Cal. 94109

CHICAGO COSTUME COMPANY
725 West Wrightwood
Chicago, Ill. 60614

CHICAGO HAIR GOODS CO. INC.
424 South Wabash Avenue
Chicago, Ill. 60605

COLUMBIA DRUG
6098 Sunset Boulevard
Los Angeles, Cal. 90028

JACK STEIN MAKEUP CENTER INC.
80 Boylston Street
Boston, Mass. 02116

KRAUSE COSTUME COMPANY
2439 Superior Avenue
Cleveland, Oh. 44114

MEYERS COSTUME SHOP
4213 Kutztown Road
Temple, Pa. 19560

NORCOSTCO INC.
3202 North Highway 100
Minneapolis, Minn. 55422

OLESON
1535 Ivar Avenue
Hollywood, Cal. 90028

PERFORMING ARTS SUPPLY COMPANY
10161 Harwin Suite 115
Houston, Tx. 77036

TECH THEATRE INC.
4724 Main Street
Lisle, Ill. 60532

THEATRICAL SERVICE AND SUPPLY INC.
170 Oval Drive
Central Islip, N.Y. 11722

WIGS—COSTUME HOUSE, INC.
8200½ Menaul N.E.
Albuquerque, N.M. 87110

12

Makeup Products

These are virtually thousands of makeup products manufactured for use in the entertainment industry. They range from traditional items, such as greasepaints and pancake, which are carried by all of the leading companies, to an array of diversified products, which are unique to each manufacturer's line. Specialized products for skin care, glues, false moustaches, aging liquids, and novelty items such as tattoos and glitter are even available. One cannot imagine any cosmetic need that cannot be filled by the range of innovative products being offered by theatrical manufacturers today. The following paragraphs introduce some of these products, old and new, and give some hints as to their use and practicality.

Greasepaints

The oldest standard of the theatre is, of course, greasepaint. It has been the staple of the theatrical world for over a century. Although largely replaced by pancake and cream-based products, it still retains its popularity with some performers. With the exception of Kryolan's liquid greasepaint, which is made primarily for underwater shows, greasepaints are manufactured in two forms: a very soft consistency, which comes in tubes like toothpaste, and a firmer

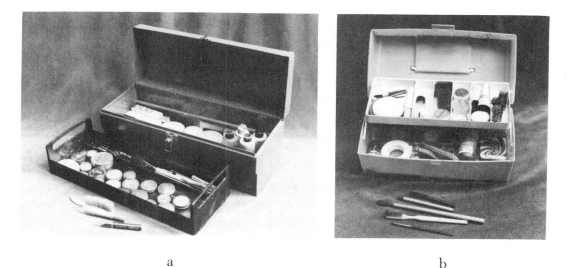

a

b

Figure 12–1.
Tool or tackle boxes can often be purchased on sale to provide handy and convenient storage for makeup and accessories.

Figure 12–2.

type available in stick form. Both have tremendous covering power and are particularly useful when used to cover buildups of wax or putties. Greasepaints are probably the least expensive of makeups available today and apply with ease. The face must be clean and prepared with a layer of cold cream. This is thoroughly wiped off and the greasepaint is applied in "dots" to the face (Figure 12–3). The fingertips are then used to blend these dots into a smooth surface.

Figure 12–3.

Figure 12–4.
Powders such as these help stop perspiration and "set" heavy makeup. Powders come in a variety of colors as well as neutral.

The drawbacks of this type of makeup, however, are many. Because greasepaints encourage perspiration, the final makeup must be "set" with powder. Using a soft puff, powder is applied liberally to the face and absorbed by the surface cosmetic. Excess is lightly brushed off with a very soft-bristled brush created for this purpose (Figure 12–5). When an actor perspires profusely, even powdering doesn't always help, and the makeup can take on a shiny look and run or rub off on a convenient costume. Because of the grease base, it does not easily come out of fabrics, human hair, or the skin. Liquifying removers or cold creams are necessary to completely cleanse the face, and even then complexion problems may result from repeated use on sensitive skins.

Figure 12–5.

Colors can be mixed easily when one wants to create an unavailable flesh tone by mixing two or more existing colors. On the other hand, controlled blending on the face is sometimes difficult. People tend to apply greasepaint rather thickly, making the precise blending of highlights and shadows a frustrating endeavor for some. If the color is not applied with great control, the face can end up with a distinctly muddy appearance.

Greasepaints are available (often with powders or pancake colors to match) from most of the leading suppliers in a wide range of tones. Kyrolan alone carries more than 250.

Pancakes

Pancake-type makeups are perhaps the most popular for use on the stage today. Pancake is a dry makeup in cake form, which is applied to the face and body with a damp sponge. The advantages of pancake are its ease of application and smooth, dry finish. Cream liners or even greasepaints can be used for highlighting and shadow work over pancake without smearing or softening the dry base. Pan-

Figure 12–6.

cakes, being water-soluble, wash out of costumes and off the face easily. Because it is essentially a dry pressed powder, colors cannot be mixed, however, and, as a base, pancake does not always hold up well (although it is an easy matter to retouch smudged or streaked areas). Powder is not necessary to set this makeup, but it can be used if necessary. A fixer, such as the type offered by Kryolan, can be purchased and sprayed on to set and seal the finished makeup.

All of the major manufacturers of makeup offer an extensive range of pancake colors in series matched for television, film, video tape, and theatrical use. Mehron and Kelly offer a series formulated especially for the black actor, while Nye goes one step further to offer colors selected for the Indian and Mexican complexion as well. Kryolan's "aquacolor" and Kelly's "rainbarrel" pancakes are of an exceptionally heavy base, which provides excellent coverage.

Figure 12–7.

Cream sticks are rapidly growing in popularity because they combine the best aspects of both greasepaints and pancake. The manufacturers promote them under various names including "velvet stick," "pan-stick," or "cream blend," but all are essentially a fairly firm stick of color with a cream base in a push-up or twist-up cylindrical tube. Applied directly to the face in a series of smears (Figure 12–9) and then blended together with the fingers, cream liners provide a smooth base of even coverage. They can be mixed together in the palm to create new colors, and they are largely absorbed by the skin, creating a dryer, flatter look than can be attained with greasepaints. Most manufacturers offer an extensive array of flesh tones as well as bright colors, some matched to their line of pancakes and powders as well.

Figure 12–9.

Figure 12–8.

170

Steins, Mehron, Factor, and Kryolan offer a line of quality liquid makeups. Basically a mixture of powder and a suspending agent (Jergens lotion can be added for better suspension), liquids dry flat and are most useful when large areas of the exposed body need to be covered. (It takes approximately three ounces per body.) The liquids come in basic flesh tones as well as intense colors, and they are applied, after vigorous shaking, with a damp sponge. One can buff and blend with the hand to help dry and smooth, since liquids are prone to streaking. Steins, who offers liquids in quarts and gallons as well as in smaller quantities, corresponds its liquid colors to its line of soft paints and panchromatic makeups.

Figure 12–10.

Figure 12–11.

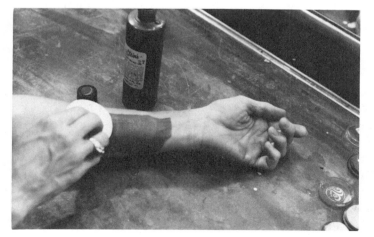

Information on cream liners, which are manufactured by all the leading makeup companies, is available in Chapter 6 on color application. To reiterate briefly, liners are available in dozens of bright lively hues. They smooth on evenly and wash off with soap and water. Generally they are used for accents and toning, but this book advocates their use exclusively for creating the base complexion as well.

Figure 12–12.

Sponges

Though cream liners and cream sticks are initially applied with the fingers, a stipple sponge is used to texture the final makeup, adding depth and additional color. The stipple sponge is a nonporous nylon sponge. The color is picked up by a multitude of relatively stiff points and transferred in the form of tiny dots to the face. Chapter 6 discusses the many advantages that can be obtained with one of these wonderful little applicators.

A natural sponge is an important addition to the makeup kit when one is applying pancake or liquid makeups. A less expensive sponge or red rubber sponge is often substituted, however—or a traditional cellulose sponge, since it is often more readily available. Red rubber sponges and natural sponges are both useful for texturing the final makeup, particularly in creating the thin blotchy look that often accompanies old age. The red rubber sponge is also recommended for applying rubber mask grease (a special greasepaint) to latex prosthetics.

Figure 12–13.

Brushes

Brushes are as important to the makeup artist as they are to the easel painter (Figure 12–14). There are brushes manufactured for combing moustaches and eyebrows, brushes for stippling, brushes for applying details, brushes for removing powder, and brushes for shading. There are brushes of squirrel hair, ox hair, sable and synthetic fibers, brushes with flat ferrules and round ferrules, and brushes with long handles or short handles. Many are manufactured for one specific purpose, while others serve dual assignments. It would be lovely if one could include one of each kind in a makeup kit, but that would end up being a rather expensive venture. Actually, only several brushes are needed, with some being used in a dual role. A toothbrush, for instance, can be used to comb eyebrows or moustaches, as well as for applying coloring to the temples or hair, thus taking the place of three separate brushes. A

Figure 12–14.

hair brush or comb is, of course, necessary, as is a soft bristle brush for powdering if one uses greasepaints. Brushes with a flat metal ferrule, preferrably in sable hair, are indispensible for both feathering and lining. A wide flat arrangement of bristles provides both a flat surface for gently feathering makeup and a very thin edge which, when used with control, effectively replaces the need for a soft pointed brush such as the Chinese water color brush. The half- and quarter-inch size are most useful, though many people prefer the eighth-inch size for detail work. An inexpensive camel hair watercolor brush (size 10, 11, or 12) is excellent for applying color to delicate tissue buildups with glues (see Figure 12–31b) or for applying light glues, latex, or collodion. A more rigid synthetic hair is more useful for spirit gum or sealers. Always wash out your brushes in water or the appropriate solvent *immediately* after using them, and store them where the bristles won't be bent and broken. Once the ferrule gets clogged with makeup or glues, the bristles lose their elasticity and control in application is lost. When working with liquid latex, always keep a jar of soapy water handy. If latex is allowed to dry in the bristles (and this takes only a matter of seconds sometimes), the brush will be ruined. Only with a *great* amount of effort can the dried rubber be pulled from bristles, and then only when they are of very stiff hog hair or a firm synthetic.

Brushes are available from Steins, Nye, Mehron, and Kryolan.

Pencils

Eyebrow pencils have been used for many years to darken eyebrows and to create wrinkles. Today, most manufacturers produce them in many colors. Playbill Cosmetics, a subsidiary of Ideal Wig Company, makes nearly forty shades of flesh tones and vibrant colors. The standard diameter is, of course, offered for use on the eyes and eyebrows, as well as a jumbo size that has the consistency of a cream stick. (Figure 12–16). The bright colors can be drawn directly on the face for stylized application, the flesh tones can be blended on the face for a base, or both can be mixed in the palm to attain additional color combinations. The pencils are wooden with a

Figure 12–15.

Figure 12–16.

plastic top and can be sharpened with a special size pencil sharpener or an X-acto knife.

Standard grease pencils can be obtained from any art supply and are useful for clown or stylized makeups. They go on smoothly and come off easily with cold cream or soap and water.

The various types of pencils that are available are shown in Figure 12–15.

Street Stuff

All the major manufacturers of stage makeup offer an assortment of items that are normally associated with street makeup, and they are necessary to add the finishing touches to many realistic applications. They include mascaras, rouges, blushes, dry eye shadow, false eyelashes, and lipsticks which can be conveniently procured at your local dime or drugstore, as well as ordered from theatrical suppliers (Figure 12–17). Many of these commercially available products, especially the Max Factor line, are of high quality and hold up well for stage use.

In addition to these "basics," each of the manufacturers of theatrical cosmetics offers an extensive line of related items for completing the makeup job in a thorough, professional manner. Applying a base of grease, cream, or pancake is certainly not the end of the makeup process—nor is it often the beginning.

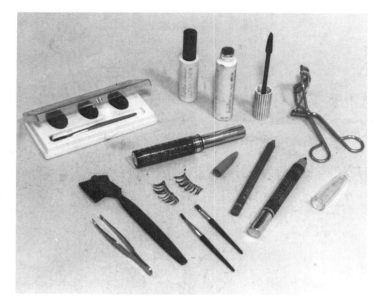

Figure 12–17.

Premakeup Preparations

Frequently a situation arises where the face must be somehow prepared before the actual makeup is applied. Using cold creams on the face before employing greasepaint is one example. People with oily complexions often use an astringent like Sea Breeze or alcohol to dry their skin, or they mix the latter one to three parts water when sponging on pancake or liquid makeups. Moisture lotions are available commercially and from theatrical suppliers, and they are useful as a base for any cosmetic application.

Occasionally a form of "cover-up" is necessary. Nye's "Five-O-Sharp" effectively covers unwanted beard stubble. Kryolan produces "Erase" in lipstick form that provides good matte coverage of blemishes, as does Kelly's "Blot-Out" available in three shades. For skin with a distinct reddish tone, either from broken surface vessels or a bad sunburn, Nye's "Mellow Yellow" is the answer. Steins "Blemi-Cream" is made to cover freckles and birthmarks. Steins also produces a "Black Eye Paint" that will eliminate all evidence of a bad night on the town.

176

At the other end of the performance, we find makeup removers. Cold creams, including Albolene, which has been used in the theatre for decades, can be procured at a drug or dime store. In addition, specialized removers are available from all of the manufacturers. Liquifying products, which dissolve greasepaints effectively, include two products from Mehron, Paramount's "Aquacreme," "Abschminke" by Leichner, and a cream from Steins that will remove spirit gum as well. Kryolan and Kelly both offer a variety of products (nonalcoholic) that are especially created for sensitive skins. Kellys, in addition to being a gentle remover, dissolves spirit gum as well. Though creams and liquid removers aid in the quick and complete removal of cosmetics, pancake, liquid, and cream-based makeups can easily be removed with simply soap and water.

Figure 12–18.

177

The hair should not be overlooked when designing makeup, so integral is its framing position to the face. Often it is covered completely with a wig (Kelly is the only manufacturer to offer custom services in wig construction, though wigs are available through many of the listed theatrical suppliers and costume houses). On other occasions, it is curled, straightened, plucked, shaved, colored, or bleached to attain the desired effect. Combs (Figure 12–19) and brushes for styling, irons for curling, hair pins for securing, nets and sprays for holding, along with dozens of other useful items, are readily available to help make these transformations.

In addition, colorants for the hair are produced by all of the manufacturers. Gone are the days of powdering with corn starch or talc when at the slightest touch the leading actress would explode in a hazy ball of dust. Leichner offers a professional powder that easily brushes into the hair, as well as a spray that comes in no less than ten colors. Like Paramount's "Color Sprae" and Kryolan's spray, which comes in 24 colors, Leichner's washes out easily with mild shampoo. Liquids, which can be applied with a sponge, toothbrush, or hair brush are provided by Nye, Mehron, Stein, Kelly, and Kryolan. Kelly and Kryolan make graying colors in a stick form as well as liquid. Liquid mascara and white pancake may also be used in altering the hair coloring.

Figure 12–19.

Figure 12–20.

Altering the Teeth

Graying, matted hair, hanging in tangled fingers over a scarred pock-marked face of swarthy complexion conjures up a wonderful image befitting a pirate or hardened criminal of days of yore. What a disappointment it would be if, when this gnarled character

Figure 12–21.

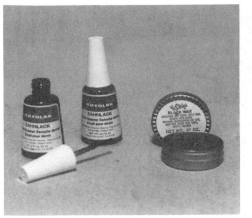

opened his mouth to speak, two rows of pearly teeth shone from between cracked lips. The teeth are often overlooked when designing makeup, thus ignoring a plausibly potent statement about the character in question. False dentures can certainly be fabricated with dental plastics, which involves some time and expertise. On the other hand, effective changes can be made with tooth wax, available from Kelly or Mehron. This wax can be heated by holding it in the hand or placing it near a light bulb until pliable. It is then pressed into a very thin sheet and modeled over teeth which have been thoroughly dried to assure adhesion. From a short distance, the teeth look chipped or rotted and can be made to disappear entirely (Figures 12–22a and b). Another approach to altering the performer's teeth is painting them (Figure 12–22c). Kryolan makes a tooth enamel in black (as does Leichner), as well as an array of colors that can be painted directly and harmlessly on the teeth. Hues include red, brown, nicotine, ivory, and white.

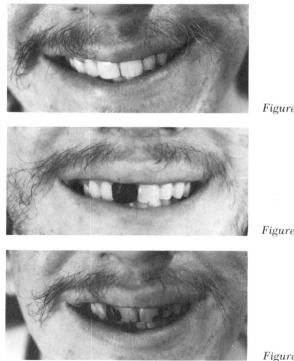

Figure 12–22a.

Figure 12–22b.

Figure 12–22c.

Three-Dimensional Products

Three-dimensional or special effects are a lot of fun to create and encompass an ever-expanding array of materials. Some, like waxes and putties, have been used for decades, dancing their way across the stage in the form of noses, chins, warts, and your basic lumps and bumps. Others, like "Glatzan" or "Tuplast" (both plastic products), are more recently developed for theatrical use.

Waxes, of course, include the tooth waxes just mentioned, moustache wax (available from Factor in white, brown, or black) for shaping and holding natural, synthetic, and crepe hair, and modeling waxes for creating various features on the face. Sometimes called "stage wax" or "mortician's wax" (since it is also used by undertakers), modeling wax is available from the various makeup companies under a variety of names: "Derma Wax," "molding wax," "nose and scar wax." Paramount's "Naturo Plasto" is available in both soft and firm consistencies, and Kryolan's "Plastici" is actually a transparent plastic product with a special wax composition. Regardless of the manufactured name, the color, which ranges from white to pink, or the manner in which it is marketed (stick or in a tin), waxes need to be kept cool. If left near a source of heat such as a light bulb, the wax will become too soft and tacky to work with. The heat of the hand is sufficient to soften them to a workable consistency.

Figure 12–23.

Virtually any shape can be created in wax, whether it be a pointed nose or a large festering wound (Figures 12–24a through d). Greasepaint colors can be gently kneaded into the wax to provide a basic complexion tone. Because waxes are not inherently sticky, many performers find that their wax nose is prone to falling off into the leading lady's dress when they bend to kiss her, a wart sticks on the scenery when they lean against it, or a chin slides slowly downward as they perspire. To avoid an embarrassing moment, adhere the wax piece to the face with a coat of spirit gum. Allow both surfaces to dry until the adhesive is slightly tacky and firmly press the wax prosthetic in place. Then simply blend the wax carefully onto the adjacent skin and apply makeup (**Figures** 12–25a through g). A piece of thread, carefully pulled between the face and the wax, will make for clean removal of the wax. The spirit gum may be removed with acetone, alcohol, or spirit gum remover. Waxes can also be used to block out the eyebrows. Kryolan makes an "Eyebrow Plastic" especially for this purpose.

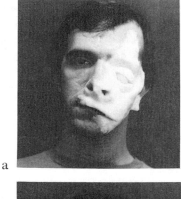

a

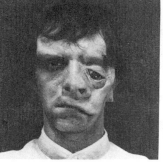

b

Figure 12–24.
This wax prosthetic is effective when viewed, but would be very impractical for a speaking part. The wax is inflexible over animated areas, and would loosen without extreme caution when the actor spoke.

c

d

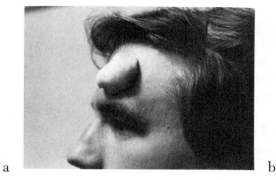
a

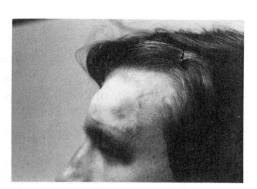
b

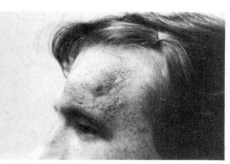
c

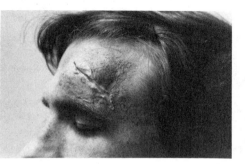
d

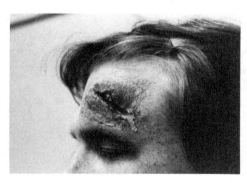
e

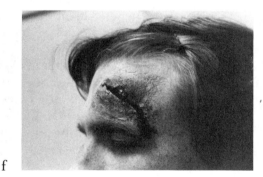
f

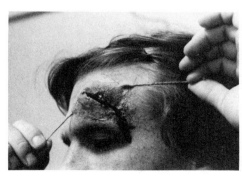
g

Figure 12–25.
These photographs illustrate a step-by-step
process of creating a wound on the face. A ball of
wax is applied to the face with spirit gum (covering
both surfaces and dried to a "tacky" state), and
smoothed into the skin. Makeup is applied, and a
"gash" is cut into the wax. The gash and
surrounding area are textured with a stipple
sponge and dark purple colors approximating a
bruise, and stage blood is syringed into the
furrow. The entire piece can be removed easily by
pulling a piece of thread or fish line between the
face and the wax to separate them. Spirit gum
remover or acetone will then clean off the residue.

183

By itself, nose putty is often difficult to manipulate because of its tacky quality, and it may be combined with wax for a better consistency by either working the two in the hands or melting them together over a double boiler. Once a putty piece has been "plastered" to the skin surface, it cannot be guaranteed to stick with the actor for the duration of the performance any more than wax. Heavy perspiration or abuse (like an elbow in the face) may loosen it. It is a good idea, with both waxes and putties, to create effects on a part of the face where they will be directly supported by the skull. There is little surface movement on the bridge of the nose, the forehead, and cheekbones; so pieces tend to adhere better in these areas. Trying to get either to stick for the duration of a performance on a cheek that is constantly flexing with expression and talking is difficult! Kelly offers a molding putty in both a roll and a tin, and Kryolan makes a soft and extra soft putty. The latter is very easy to mold.

There are certainly limitations to working with putties and waxes. Other than their propensity not to adhere well when used in bulk on a sweating performer, it is sometimes difficult to create a believable effect with these materials. They tend to look bulky and unnatural unless one is careful to shape them carefully and texture the surface with a stipple sponge to approximate the natural texture of adjacent flesh. Since lightweight, natural-looking noses and chins can be procured from Kryolan, Paramount, Rubies, or any number of other theatrical suppliers for a nominal fee, most theatres utilize the commercially foamed latex pieces rather than wax or putty prosthetics. They also have the advantage of being easily reused.

Foam Latex

As an option to waxes and putties, or to purchasing premade prosthetics, many theatres fabricate their own from a foam latex kit. This not only offers the advantage of custom-designed pieces, but insures a perfect fit as well. The process is not at all difficult, and it is really quite exciting to "pull" your first cast from the mold. Foam latex can be purchased from Paramount Theatrical Supply or Kryolan. Both systems include four components, which are

Figure 12–26.

frothed together with a kitchen beater to a light consistency, poured into a negative mold, and allowed to "cure." The latex sold by Paramount needs to be baked for twenty to twenty-five minutes, while the Kryolan product does not. For illustrations showing the step-by-step method for creating pliable lightweight prosthetics of a delicate skin-like texture, see Figures 12–27a through s.

Figure 12–27.

In order to make prosthetics of foamed latex, one must have a cast of his or her own face done in plaster from which to work. A likeness done in plaster is called a "positive" cast and is achieved by pouring fine grain dental plaster into a "negative" mold of the face. There are two approaches to making a negative casting. (a), (b), and (c) show the process using moulage, a rubber-like compound that is mixed in powder form with water and heated until liquified in the top of a double boiler. The thick creamy mixture is then brushed onto the face as soon as it is cool enough not to burn the skin. Moulage will not stick to facial hair or skin, and therefore can be removed with ease as soon as it is "set." Another advantage is the incredible detail that it is possible to obtain. Because of its flexibility, however, plaster bandage must be applied to the moulage for rigidity (c). Another drawback is the propensity of moulage to shrink as the moisture evaporates from the surface. Unless the casting is used immediately, proportion and detail can be lost, and within a day your lovely negative mold can revert to a tiny shrunken head that is obviously useless.

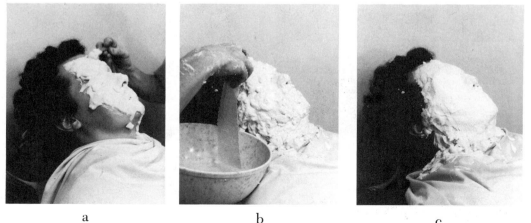

a   b   c

d

e

f

g

h

i

j

k

l

m

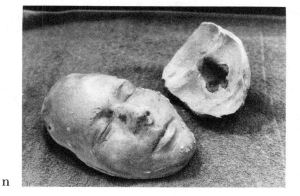

n

Figure 12–27 (cont.)
A process that provides a more permanent mold utilizes plaster, an easily obtainable and inexpensive material. Unless you want five pounds of dripping plaster in your lap, the casting process needs to be done in a near prone position, which can be a drawback as the flesh and muscles are in an unnatural position. Because of the weight of the plaster, and the fact that it gets very, very warm upon curing, the "victim" needs to be prepared for what may seem a claustrophobic experience to some people. Horror stories abound concerning plaster in eyes and mouths, facial hair being pulled out, and so forth. When done properly, however, the process is perfectly safe (though messy) and not unlike a comfortable facial treatment.

187

o

p

q

Figure 12–27 (cont.)
After preparing the actor physiologically, it is important to prepare him or her physically for a plaster casting. This includes placing a release agent such as Vasaline over the entire face, including any exposed facial hair. A thin sheet of Saran Wrap or a bathing cap may be applied over the actual hair rather than greasing it. A form cut (d) of lightweight upson or masonite should fit snugly around the face to halt the flow of plaster onto the back of the head. (If a small portion of the face is needed, such as the nose or an ear, a "dike" of clay can simply be constructed around this area.) A straw may be placed in the relaxed mouth, or, after careful wrapping with cotton, placed into the nostrils. (Since the shape of the nostrils is frequently altered by the latter method, and the nose is most frequently utilized for prosthetics, the mouth is recommended.) Ample air can be drawn through a single straw, though some people may prefer two. Once the person is thoroughly relaxed and a system of hand signals has been determined (since it is very difficult to talk with a pile of plaster on your face), the plaster may be mixed and applied (e). Directions accompany plaster to assure proper mixing and setting, so be sure to follow them carefully. If the composition is too thin, it will simply run off the face. If it is too thick, bubbles and air holes will develop and a detailed cast will be almost impossible. The first application should be rather thin and "tapped" onto the skin to release bubbles and assure accurate details. Note in (f) that plaster has been worked around the nostrils, leaving them free for breathing. The second application (g) utilizes the plaster that is now relatively thick (too thick to run into the nostrils, for instance) and follows the first application immediately. The plaster will set in a matter of four to eight minutes. By simply moving the facial muscles, the material is released from the skin and the mold can be easily removed (h). Allow

188

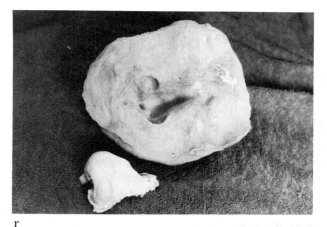

r

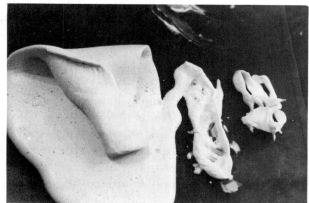

s

the negative mold to set for a day or two until the moisture has evaporated from the plaster. Any irregularities or air bubbles can be filled in with clay. Coat the negative mold with Vasaline or liquid latex to insure easy removal, and fill the cavity with plaster. Run a knife blade slowly through the wet material to release any air bubbles that may have been trapped, insert a bent hanger while the plaster is still in a liquid state (to aid in removal), and allow the plaster to set until the plaster is thoroughly set and dry (one or two days is usually sufficient). Using the hanger to help pull, separate the negative from the positive and you should have a flawless likeness of the performer. This plaster form can now be used as a basic armature for constructing any prosthetic feature on the face. (k) shows a nose built of clay over the positive mold. (l) and (m) show plaster once again being used to make a negative mold of the fabricated nose. The clay nose can still be seen in (n), showing the plaster after drying and removal from the positive facial cast. Clean all of the clay from the negative and again apply a release agent. After mixing a batch of foamed latex according to the accompanying directions, pour it into the negative cavity (p) originally occupied by the clay. Replace the plaster cast in its position on the positive (q) and bake the latex approximately 20 minutes. The foamed latex will "cure" in the oven and assume a flexible rubber form. Once cooled, separate the two plaster casts, and remove the resulting latex prosthetic (r). Trim the edges, apply makeup, and it will fit perfectly over the actor's own nose. (s) shows excess foamed latex that was simply poured into a sheet of foil and baked. Excellent scars, wounds, and special effects can be fabricated from this extra material.

189

Liquid latex, quite a different product from the foamed variety, is essentially a liquid rubber that is meant to be used directly from the bottle. It is available in pink or white, dries relatively clear, and can be ordered from Kelly, Paramount, and Kryolan. Liquid latex dries to form a sheet of flexible, durable rubber, making it a useful product for a variety of assignments. When applied to a plaster mold, it performs as a release agent when casting. The liquid bonds well to the foamed variety, providing a surface skin that is sometimes desirable on the prosthetic being cast. Liquid latex can be used as a glue to adhere moustaches, scars, and the like, but it tends to "float" from the skin surface if the performer perspires heavily. When applied in several coats, liquid latex makes an excellent backing for beards or moustaches when working with crepe hair (Figure 12–41f). The tough rubber allows the entire piece to be peeled off the skin in one unit and reused. Latex, combined with tissue, cord, bits of sawdust, or what-have-you, is often used to create wonderful wounds, gashes, or scars (Figures 12–29a and b). The benefits of using latex over putties or waxes are, of course, its durability and longevity. The scar can be carefully peeled away from the face at the conclusion of the evening's performance, placed on a mirror or sheet of glass to protect it from abuse, and reapply it with spirit gum for the next night's show. Waxes, on the other hand, often need to be reshaped and blended into the skin, taking time away from other preparation and with no guarantee of perfection from night to night. Figures 12–30a through d show build-ups being done with tissue and cotton. Though collodion or liquid

Figure 12–28.

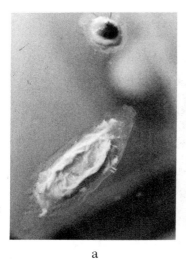

a   b

Figure 12–29.

a   b

Figure 12–30.

c   d

191

sealer is sometimes used for this type of three-dimensional work, it is not as satisfactory to work with as latex. Figures 12–31a and b show how to create dimensional wrinkles with latex and tissue. Similar effects can be achieved with other products as well. Kryolan's "Old Skin Plat" is applied to the skin one portion at a time while the surface is being stretched tautly. When dry, the skin appears to wrinkle, giving a subtle effect of aging. Unlike latex, which can be removed and saved, Old Skin Plat is dissolved with acetone. Nye's "Old Age Plastic and Sealer" gives similar results. While Nye's product doubles as a fixative to seal makeup on the face or prosthetic pieces, thereby helping to retain color and shape, Kryolan's product does not. Kryolan does, however, make both a liquid and a spray sealer, which, like Nye's, can be used over latex.

Figure 12–31.
The hands shown in (c) and (d) are both effectively aged, though they read quite differently. Simple shading has been employed to create the dimension on figure (d), which would read quite believably from a distance. The hand in figure (c) however, with its three-dimensional application, would read from any angle and distance as aged, and is usually a more effective approach to solving an assignment of advanced age.

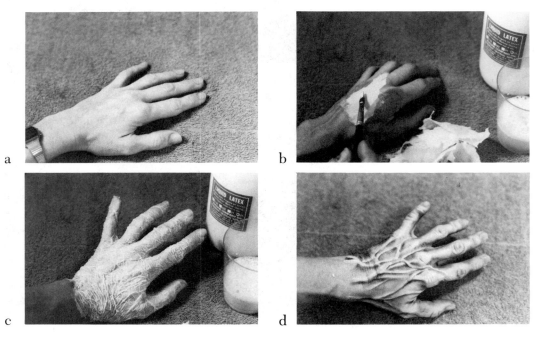

a

b

c

d

Latex prosthetics can be painted with rubber mask grease or even with latex or acrylic paints. Latex should not be used on anyone who is allergic to makeup or has sensitive skin. An inexpensive substitute for latex in making buildups is flexible glue such as Sobo or Swifts. This harmless adhesive can be thinned to a workable consistency (about three parts glue to one water) and is as effective as Latex for class projects or for one-time performances. Since it does not dry with the same flexibility as Latex, it cannot be reused. Figures 12–32a and b shows an old age makeup done with glue and tissue. Kryolan's water base colors, liquid makeup, or even acrylic or watercolors can be used to color the buildups with glue while they are still damp. The texture of the tissue provides a subtle bleeding together of the colors that greatly enhances the delicate quality. Once dry, greasepaints or cream sticks may be used.

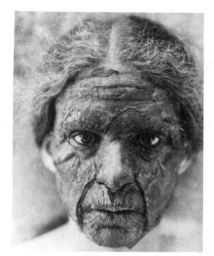

a

Figure 12–32.
This aging project was completed with tissue and glue. Note the stark contrast between the ears and neck as compared with the face proper. Such applications read with exceptional clarity, and when applied with minimal layers, move and flex naturally with the performer's expressions. (b) shows a closeup of the texture obtainable with tissue and glue (or latex). Note how closely it approximates actual wrinkled flesh.

b

A word of caution: Latex is very difficult to remove from the hair or eyebrows. It is a good idea to soap or wax these areas if latex will make contact with them.

Speaking of Scars . . .

There are several additional products especially designed for creating scars, surface abrasions, or wounds (Figures 12–33a through c). Kelly makes a scarring liquid, and Paramount sells nonflexible collodion which serves the same purpose. Kryolan's "Tuplast" is a harmless plastic that is removed with acetone. In addition, they offer "Plasti-bond," a special tape that can be formed into scars.

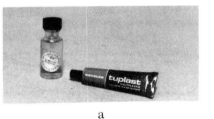

Figure 12–33.

a

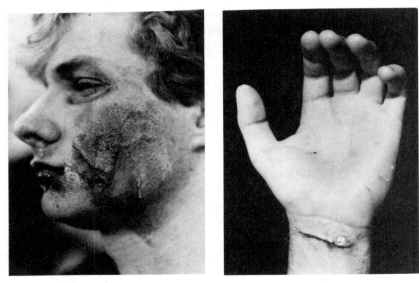

b　　　　　　　　c

Library paste and scotch tape are hardly appropriate materials for attaching prosthetics to the face. Special adhesives have been formulated specifically for this purpose. Spirit gum is an old favorite in the theatre because of its strength. Each of the manufacturers offers spirit gum in their line, each differing in strength and drying time. Spirit gum may be used for sticking down eyebrows, pinning the ears back, securing false hair to the face or attaching latex, putty, or wax pieces to the face (Figure 12–34). A matte finish spirit gum, produced by Kryolan, is recommended for work at the hairline or wherever the glue might show, since regular spirit gum dries with a somewhat shiny finish. Spirit gum must be removed with acetone, alcohol, spirit gum remover, or special makeup creams sold by Kelly and Steins.

Surgical adhesives, which again can be purchased at a drug counter, are perfectly safe for such items as false eyelashes, and they are suggested for very sensitive skin. Nye's "Wiggums Adhesive," Kelly's "Matte Adhesive," and Paramount's "Slomon's Medico Adhesive" are all excellent for attaching premade beards, moustaches, and lightweight prosthetics.

Specialty adhesives include a "Beard Stubble Adhesive Stick" by Kelly and Kryolan's "Stipplepaste." Both provide a tacky surface to which bits of crepe hair will stick, creating a delightful unshaven appearance.

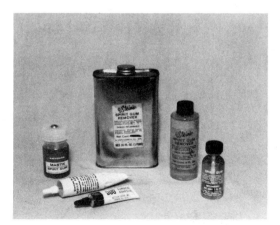

Figure 12–34.

195

The proper placement of hairpieces and wigs requires a stick-um of a different nature. Though Kelly produces an undetectable liquid toupee adhesive, tapes have a corner on the market. Kelly and Paramount both sell adhesive tapes, as does Kryolan. In addition, the latter offers double-sided adhesive strips, film and fabric to help secure bald caps as well as wigs. Kryolan also manufactures a matte finish plastic tape that effectively blends the edge of bald caps and wigs.

Though certainly not useful for adhering hair, standard surgical tape is also a handy addition to the makeup kit. It can be used for transforming deep-set Caucasian eyes into those with a more Oriental configuration (Figures 12–35a through f).

Figure 12–35.
Surgical tape is cut to fit over the actress's own eyelid in such a way as to seemingly alter the actual shape of her eye. Liquid latex is applied at the edges to help create a smooth, clean transition between the tape and the actual skin. When dry, makeup is applied, the actual eyebrow is blocked out with wax, and a new one lined in with a brush. From a short audience distance, the effect appears flawless.

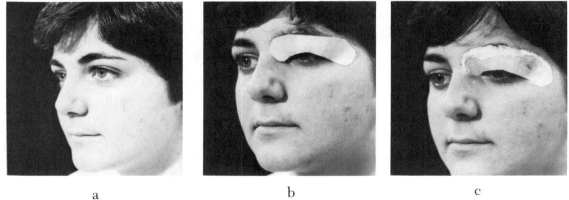

a   b   c

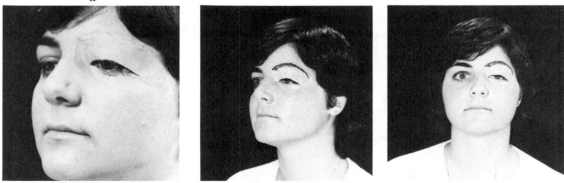

d   e   f

Bald caps can be ordered from Paramount as well as from several other theatrical houses (Figure 12–36). Kryolan not only offers bald caps, but a liquid and aerosol plastic called "Glatzan" which can be applied to forms enabling makeup artists to create their own rigidless caps. They also provide a matte finish that helps bald caps take makeup more readily and a dye for coloring Glatzan. If you're in a pinch, a thin swimming cap may be used, though one must often mask the bulky edge with tape or latex (Figures 12–37a and b).

Figure 12–36.

Figure 12–37.

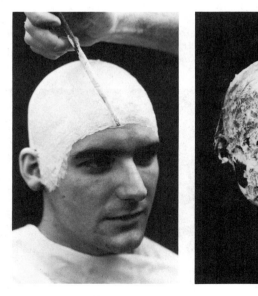

a   b

197

Figure 12–38.

When done with care, the effects of baldness or of a receding hairline can be effectively created by using soap to modify the natural hairline. Figures 12–39a through g show a step-by-step process.

Figure 12–39.
Though soap flakes may be softened in water overnight, small bars of guest soap, half submerged for eight to twenty hours (depending upon the brand) are more convenient to work with since they provide a firm end to hold. The hair is done one portion at a time, making sure each layer is sufficiently smoothed and soaped before pulling another layer over the top to be soaped. A hair dryer is useful for hardening each subsequent layer. Once the desired area has been thoroughly saturated and smoothed, a nylon stocking is cut to fit and stretched over the soaped area. Spirit gum is used to affix it to the forehead, after which it is stretched back over the "bald" area to provide texture and a foundation that will readily accept makeup.

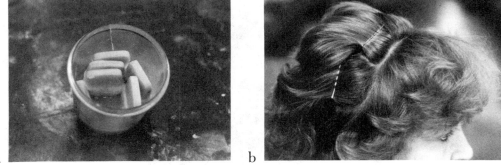

a   b

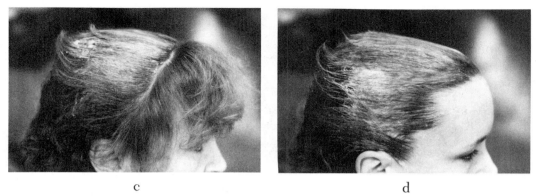

c

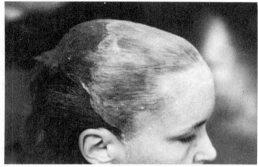

d

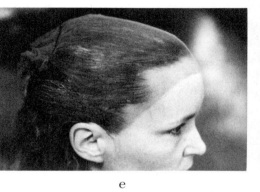

e

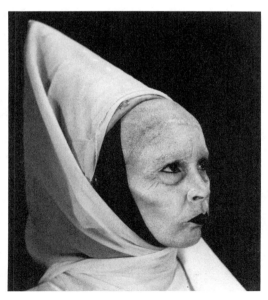

f

g

Altering or supplementing the natural hair can be accomplished in one of several ways. A bit of research will show you that hairstyles have shifted from plain to outrageous and back again throughout history. Many styles can easily be duplicated on an actor or actress with colorants, curlers, or a curling iron. Others, like the piled wigs of the seventeenth century, must be conceived artificially. Custom-made wigs can be ordered from Kelly, while standard period wigs can be ordered from Paramounts, Rubies, and many costume suppliers. You may even be able to find something suitable at a local wig shop. Most cities have an establishment that will hand-make toupees or wigs as well. Another alternative is making one's own wig. Paramount sells netting materials and synthetic blends of hair in dynel, saran, or nylon for hand-tying wigs.

Facial hair is a problem that is often much easier to accommodate. Crepe hair, available by the foot or yard, is perhaps the most popular route as it is inexpensive and relatively easy to work with. Figures 12–41a through j and Figures 12–42a through d show step-by-step procedures for creating hair where none exists.

a

Figure 12–40
Moustaches such as this one, in which the hairs are stitched onto a net backing, can be procured for only a few dollars from many theatrical suppliers. It can be shaped with moustache wax and used indefinitely with proper care.

b

200

Figure 12–41.
The materials necessary for making a moustache or beard include crepe hair, scissors, tweezers, and spirit gum. If the piece is to be reusable, liquid latex is necessary as well. Crepe hair is available by the foot or the yard in a tight braid. Many colors can be purchased, from natural hues to bright clown red. The hair should be unbraided, and at least 60 percent of the "kink" removed. This can be done by soaking the hair and wrapping it in a towel to dry, or simply using a steam iron to remove the desired degree of curl. After cutting it into lengths of approximately six inches, comb the hair to remove loose or short strands. This can be accomplished by holding one end firmly while combing and then reversing ends. Cut the hair into the desired length and select two or more colors appropriate for the beard or moustache being fabricated. As you can see in (d), facial hair is often irregular in color, of a hue that doesn't match the hair, and veriegated within itself. If you look closely at your own hair, you will find a variety of colors from strand to strand. It is this variety that lends a lifelike quality. A moustache composed of a single color will indeed look phony on the face. Once your colors are selected, combine them carefully by overlapping and pulling apart between the fingers until the strands are thoroughly mixed. (e) indicates areas and sequence of application for a typical full beard. Note that you begin at the chin, working along the lower edge of the jaw first. The subsequent application covers the first. If the beard or moustache is not a one-time application, several layers of latex (f) are necessary to create a flexible and removeable foundation. Allow complete drying time between each application. Spirit gum is then used to affix the actual hair over the latex. Apply the spirit gum to one area at a time and allow it to dry until just tacky. Take a small bundle of crepe hair in the hand and fluff it out to avoid thick, unnatural gobs of growth on the face. Trim at an angle and remove loose and stray hairs. Holding the bundle at a 90° angle to the face, gently push the tips into the spirit gum (g). A brush handle may be used to press stray ends, and a towel may be gently pressed against the bundle to assure adhesion. Continue from area to area, applying a small bundle to each. When the entire area has been covered and allowed to dry, gently brush out stray hairs, comb, and trim to the desired shape. (i) indicates a thick Norse beard that would read well from a distance. (j), however, shows a more modern version for close-play situations. The secret to this type of application is a cautious control of both spirit gum and hair application, allowing a natural, veriegated edge against the skin. A few hairs at a time may need to be applied to create a "natural" look.

a

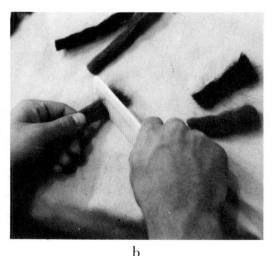

b

c

Figure 12–41 (cont.)

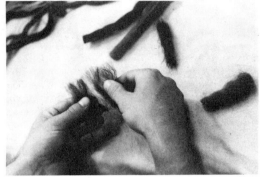

d

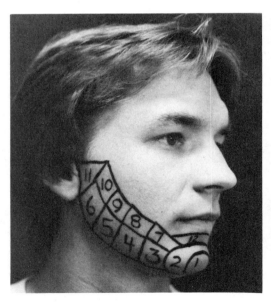

e

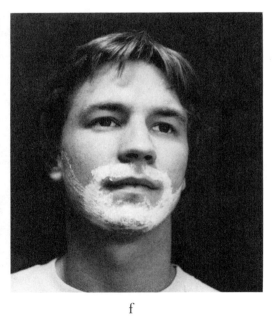

f

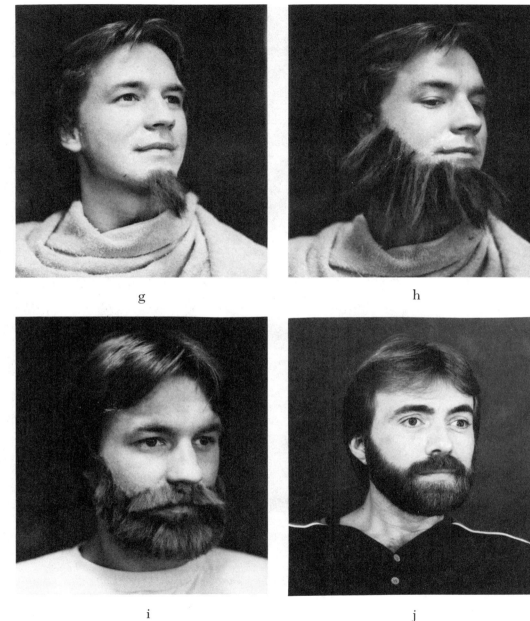

g

h

i

j

Figure 12–42.
(a) illustrates placement and sequence for the application of crepe hair in constructing a moustache. Combing and combining the hairs is of course identical in process to beard construction. Begin with the outer edges and work in toward the philtrum. (c) shows the finished moustache in rather long form, while (d) shows the same application trimmed to a short style. Because this project was not for an extended run of a show, no latex was used as a base. The spirit gum was applied directly to the skin and was dissolved later with spirit gum remover.

In addition to these popular products, there are numerous items manufactured for special effects. With all the violence so popular in the media at present, where would we be without stage blood? Though Steins and Kelly both offer a blood, Steins does not wash out of costumes well and Kelly's comes only in "artery" color.

"Nextel" stage blood is available from both Paramount and Nye. Created by the 3-M company, it is considered one of the superior bloods on the market. Its primary advantage is its washability. It is nontoxic and can be thinned with water or thickened with a water-base clear hair grooming gel.

Kryolan has several types of stage blood on the market. A special nondrying blood comes in light and dark shades. A paste form, available in a tube, dries very quickly and is removable with acetone. A slow-drying jelly is available, as well as an artificial blood, which can be used for special effects. The bloody effect is noticeable only when two components combine. Kryolan offers other bloods suitable for internal consumption in capsule, gel, and liquid form. Paramount and Kryolan both provide blood capsules and blood bags which can be placed strategically in the clothing or held in the mouth. With a selection like this, there is no excuse for homemade formulas of Karo, chocolate syrup, food coloring, and corn starch that inevitably stains costumes. Save it for ice cream topping.

Figure 12–43.
These photos illustrate an application of crepe hair that reads quite unbelievably. The hairs seem to sprout from random directions, have a tenuous quality that makes one expect them to fall out, and retain a ragged look. It takes a lot of practice and patience to apply crepe hair so that it is accepted as real by the audience.

a   b

205

When the effect you want is fantasy or fantastic, don't overlook makeups that glow in the dark only when lights hit them or under black light. Each can be an exciting addition to a production number. Steins offers green in both fluorescent and phosphorescent mixtures. Leichner manufacturers luminescent makeup in green, blue, yellow, and red. "Metallic" makeups have the gloss and shine of metals but do not glow in the dark. Kryolan's "Liquid Brightness" in silver, copper, and gold is actually nonmetallic in composition and is therefore ideal for sensitive skins. Kryolan's other metallic makeup is called "Satinpuder" and comes in pearl, yellow, silver, and gold. Mehron manufactures metallic eyeshadow and irridescent eyeshadow liners in several colors including bronze-purple and antique brown. Mehron makes both a metallic powder and "Texas Dirt" (a body powder) in silver and gold. All of the metallics provide a lovely gloss and rich highlights when used over other makeups as well, or when sprinkled or brushed into the hair.

Et Cetera

A curious assortment of other paraphernalia can be found in the catalogues and brochures supplied by the manufacturers of cosmetics for use on the stage today, including special boxes in which to keep all your makeup goodies (Figures 12–1a and b). Cosmetics for water shows, tiny tattoos, beauty marks, glitter, and a host of other cosmetics to tempt your imagination are available. Kelly even supplies "Mr. Makeup Kits," which provide the instructions and the makeup to do your favorite monsters, hobos, and witches. These will undoubtedly bring the world of theatrical makeup to "would-be" actors everywhere . . . especially at Halloween, when everyone envies the makeup artist.

Certainly history has shown us that the human animal has a fascination with makeup. There is an intrigue about transforming

206

one's face in front of a mirror. Whether it is a small child, wobbling in high heels and circling his mouth with mom's lipstick, a woman carefully adjusting her makeup before an evening out, or the performer transforming his face into another time and age, the illusions that can be created on the face and in the mind are somehow . . . magic.

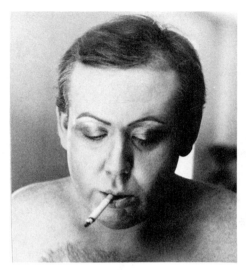

a

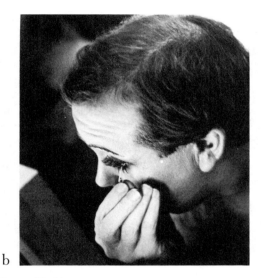

b

Figure 12–44.
One of the greatest transformations possible with theatrical makeup is changing one's sex. This actor, in The Madness of Lady Bright *had to do just that during the progression of the one-act play. The change, done entirely in front of the audience, was remarkable.*

c

Index